Rotisserie Turkey

MIKE VROBEL

Other books by Mike Vrobel

Rotisserie Grilling

Rotisserie Chicken Grilling

Version 1.02

Copyright © 2015 Mike Vrobel

Photographs copyright © 2015 Mike Vrobel

ISBN 0985512555

Thank you, Diane. All I do depends on you.

Thank you, Ben, Natalie, and Tim. I love you.

Thank you, Mom, for all those huge Thanksgiving dinners. I don't know how you do it every year.

Thank you, Dad, for trying that crazy Weber kettle turkey recipe. It started me down the path that led to this book.

Thank you to the rest of my family. I wouldn't be here without all the love and support you've given me.

Thank you to Suzanne Fass, my editor, for her hard work and watchful eye.

This book is built on all the hard work and creative ideas of those who went before me. To the world of food — writers, photographers, chefs, home cooks, farmers, ranchers, butchers, market goers, grillers and grill makers: thank you all.

ABOUT ROTISSERIE TURKEY

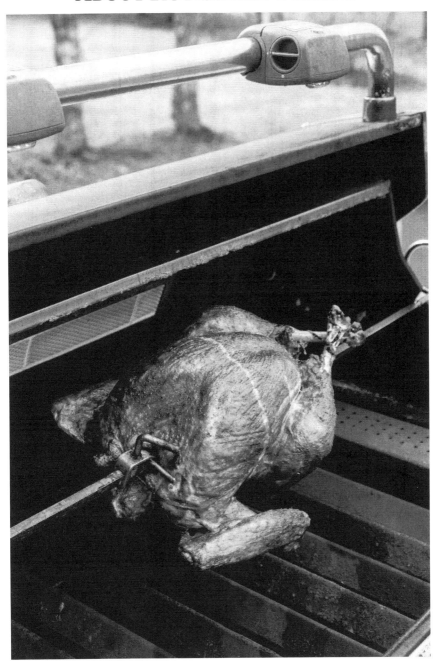

INTRODUCTION

Thanksgiving is show time for home cooks. It is our time to shine, pulling out all the stops to make a feast for family and friends.

I write about rotisserie turkey every year on my blog. In early November, the questions start. A few trickle in early in the month, asking about strategy and tactics. As T-Day approaches, the volume increases, and the questions sound more nervous. On Thanksgiving, when I'm not checking on my own turkey, I spend the day on my cell phone - responding, coaching, cajoling, and in some cases talking people down off the ledge. Trust me - your Thanksgiving turkey will be just fine.

After the turkey leftovers are done, and I've had time to recover, I gather any new questions and use them as the basis for next year's Thanksgiving blog posts.

This book is a collection of those years of blog posts and questions, cleaned up and rewritten when necessary. It gives me something to refer to when people ask questions: "Here it is, I wrote it all down in one place!"

WHY ROTISSERIE TURKEY?

I cook my Thanksgiving turkey on the grill every year; this year I'll grill two of them.

Family and friends watch me out in the cold wrestling with a 12-pound bird while they sit inside watching the Macy's parade and the football games. Someone always asks: "Why do you do this? Why grill your turkey? Why not cook it in the oven?" (with an implied "like normal people do"). Because . . .

Top Five Reasons to Rotisserie the Thanksgiving Turkey:

1. Improving Taste

Why cook anything on the grill? Because it just tastes better—and turkey needs the help, particularly turkey breast. Turkey is very lean, which means . . . bland. Needs gravy. And stuffing. That is, unless the turkey is grilled, especially on the rotisserie.

Rotisserie turkey has crisp, browned skin from the dry heat of the grill and a hint of smoky flavor to the meat. If you brine the bird first and add a little smoking wood to the fire, that can only help. (To get *real* turkey flavor, I go for the dark meat and make sure I get a drumstick every Thanksgiving.)

2. Saving Space

Thanksgiving dinner means a jumbo turkey plus stuffing, squash, green bean casserole, sweet potatoes, and dinner rolls. So Thanksgiving is as much about logistics as it is about cooking. A home kitchen is sized to cook for a single family, not for the typical Thanksgiving gathering. Do you ever wish you had a second oven on Thanksgiving? Guess what—you do, right outside on the patio. I'm serving about 20 people this Thanksgiving, and I'll be cooking two turkeys—one on my kettle grill, the other on my gas grill. I'll have plenty of room in the oven for my stuffing and side dishes.

3. Cleaning Up

Stuck scrubbing out roasting pans while everyone else snoozes on the couch in a tryptophan haze? Use the grill and cut the cleaning in half. Once the foil pan in the grill has cooled down, crumple it into a ball and toss it in to the trash. Cleanup is done!

4. Getting Out of the Kitchen

This has two parts, the practical, and the psychological. The practical part: You don't have to elbow through all the people in the kitchen to get to the bird—it's out in the backyard, where there is plenty of space. I'm not sure why, but everyone migrates into the kitchen right when crunch time happens. I have to elbow Uncle Jack out of the way to get the turkey from the oven to the cutting board.

The psychological part: You get to go outside! If you're lucky, it's a beautiful fall day and you can take a few minutes to check on the bird. Take a deep breath of crisp fall air, sip a lovely beverage, get away from the heat of the kitchen, and watch the grill for a few minutes. I live in northeastern Ohio, so my "beautiful fall day" is usually gray, 37°F, with a threat of a rain-sleet mix. I still like to get out for a few minutes. (Yes, I'm an introvert—does it show?)

5. Impressing the Guests

You want the Norman Rockwell picture of plenty on Thanksgiving? Watch what happens when you carry the beautifully grilled bird into the house on a spit. Conversations pause for a second, someone lets out a low whistle, and everyone crowds around, telling you how gorgeous the bird is. Hey, you've been working on dinner all afternoon—of course you want your ego stroked.

TEN STEPS TO ROTISSERIE TURKEY

There is extra work involved with rotisserie grilling a turkey—more than sliding it into the oven—but it's worth the extra effort. Here are the ten steps to a successful rotisserie turkey.

Before you start, you need the following (see Equipment on page 31 for more on each of these).

- A grill with a rotisserie attachment (spit, spit forks, motor, and motor mount)

- Trussing string (look for heavy butcher's twine)

- Heat proof gloves (the spit gets hot)

- Drip pan (A 9 by 12- or 13- inch grill safe pan)

- A turkey (duh)

1. Season the turkey.

This can be a simple sprinkling of salt and pepper, or an elaborate brine and spice rub combination. Don't forget it, though: There is nothing blander than unsalted turkey. See Seasoning the Bird (Page 24) for seasoning options.

2. Truss and spit the turkey.

The turkey needs to be trussed into a tight package and secured on the rotisserie spit. A rotisserie turns gently, but even gentle turning will pull the turkey loose from the spit if it is not securely tied down. See Trussing and Spitting (Page 15) for a how-to.

3. Set up the grill up for indirect medium heat, with a drip pan in the middle, and preheat to medium. The fire should be on the edges of the grill, not underneath the turkey; direct heat will burn the turkey during the long cooking time. The drip pan sits under the turkey to catch turkey juices and fat. See Gas Grill Setup (Page 19) or Charcoal Grill Setup (Page 21) for details. Medium heat is roughly 350°F.

4. Mount the motor.

Slide the rotisserie motor onto the mounting bracket, plug it in, and turn the motor on and off to make sure it is working.

5. Mount the spit into the rotisserie bracket.

Make sure the grill lid is open. Put on heatproof gloves, lift the spit and turkey, and take it out to the grill. Plug the point of the spit into the rotisserie motor. Set the notch on the spit into the groove on the other side of the grill. (The groove is in the rotisserie ring for a charcoal grill; it is built into the side of the firebox for a gas grill.)

What about the counterweight? I skip counterweights if the turkey is less than 20 pounds. If the turkey is 20 pounds or more, and the rotisserie comes with a counterweight, then I'll use it if the turkey feels unbalanced. If you want to counterweight: Remove the motor from the mounting bracket and set the spit in the grooves on the rotisserie ring. Let the spit go and gravity takes over — the turkey will rock back and forth, eventually settling with its heaviest part facing down. Attach the counterweight to the end of the spit pointing straight up, and voilà, balanced! Lift the spit out, remount the motor, remount the spit, and go.

6. Turn on the rotisserie motor.

Make sure the spit is turning freely, the turkey is secure and not bumping into any part of the grill, and the drip pan is centered below the bird. If the turkey is loose or wobbly, stop the motor, loop some string around the meat, and tie it down tight. Better to tie it down it now than to find it ripped loose from the spit forks later.

7. Cook with the lid closed.

Leave the motor running and close the lid. Cook with the lid closed as much as possible until the turkey is done. I check on the turkey every hour to make sure everything is still turning properly, then close the lid again. The turkey is done when it reaches 155°F in the thickest part of the breast and 175°F in the deepest part of the leg joint, measured with an instant-read thermometer.

8. Using heatproof gloves, remove the spit from the grill and transfer the turkey and spit to a carving board.

Be careful—the spit is a branding iron when it first comes off the grill. Bring a large carving board to the grill, lift the spit and bird out of the grill, and set the bird on the cutting board. This will catch drips as you carry the turkey into the house.

9. Remove the spit from the turkey, then remove the trussing string.

Remove the first spit fork from the spit. Using tongs or a carving fork, hold the turkey in place on the carving board while pulling the spit out of the bird. Keep your gloves on until you have the spit set down on a heatproof surface. Cut the trussing string and remove it from the turkey immediately. (The crust on the bird will harden as it cools; the sooner you get the trussing string off, the better.)

10. Rest, carve, and serve.

Let the turkey rest for 15 to 30 minutes to relax from the heat of the grill, then carve and serve.

TURKEY TROUBLES

Warning - food science geekery ahead.

One-hundred-sixty-five degrees Fahrenheit for turkey. That temperature is burned into my memory. The United States Department of Agriculture says:

> A whole turkey is safe when cooked to a minimum internal temperature of 165°F, as measured with a food thermometer.
>
> *Source: USDA "Let's Talk Turkey ""A Consumer Guide to Safely Roasting a Turkey"*

The USDA recommends 165°F to kill salmonella. If the turkey reaches 165°F, salmonella is killed in less than 10 seconds. Easy, right? Cook the turkey to 165°F and it is done. Not so fast. A temperature of 165°F is good for food safety, but it's borderline for taste.

White meat dries out easily.

Meat is a made up of protein fibers and water. The moment meat gets to 120°F (blood-red rare), the protein fibers start to tighten up, squeezing water out of the meat. At 165°F, almost all the water has been squeezed out. Fat and connective tissue can make up for this; they add their own juiciness, and break down at higher temperatures. The leaner meat is, the closer to rare you want to cook it. Turkey breast is almost all protein; it is one of the leanest meats you can buy. Ever cut into a slice of turkey breast that was dry as dust? It was overcooked. All the juices were squeezed out by the high heat.

The USDA isn't advising 165°F because they prefer dry white meat. We can't just cook turkey breast to medium-rare; it's not safe. But there is an escape clause. The USDA also has a time-temperature chart for professional food processing. Killing salmonella isn't just about temperature—it's also about time. At 165°F, salmonella is dead after 10 seconds. At 134°F (medium-rare), salmonella is killed after 64 minutes. At home, I don't have the precision cooking equipment needed to reliably hold food at 134°F. Also, I'm not cooking my poultry to medium-rare, with a warm pink center. Pink-centered poultry looks raw to me; that's unsettling.

According to the USDA time-temperature chart, at 150°F salmonella is killed in just under four minutes. If I cook my turkey breast to 150°F, measured in the deepest part of the meat, then leave it on the grill for another five minutes, I'm safe—the salmonella should be dead. Medium-well, 150°F, is my turkey breast trade-off. (Plus that extra five minutes, just in case.) Not so well done that all the water was squeezed out; cooked long enough that salmonella is not a concern.

My Samoan attorney would like me to say the following: *If you are feeding infants or people with compromised immune systems, stick with the USDA guidelines and cook turkey breast to 165°F. It's the only way to be sure.*

Dark meat needs to be overcooked.

So 150°F, then five minutes more. Great! Time to put the turkey on the spit, right?

Not so fast. Are we cooking a whole turkey? Because we've only talked about white meat so far.

Our next problem is dark meat. Turkey legs are full of fat and connective tissue. Connective tissue only starts to break down at 160°F, and the higher the temperature, the better. Ever bite into a tough, chewy drumstick? It was undercooked.

Turkey legs are best between 175° and 185°F; at that temperature, the fat melts and the connective tissues break down, leaving us with tender, juicy, easily shreddable meat.

But . . . but . . . didn't I just say that we can't overcook the breast meat? That 175°F white meat is as dry as sawdust? Are we stuck? Satisfy the white meat partisans by cooking the turkey to 150°F, and give chewy drumsticks to Uncle Phil, the dark meat fan? Or cook the turkey to 175°F, enjoy tender dark meat, and use the white meat as sandpaper?

Now, I am a dark meat kind of guy, and I always liked Uncle Phil, but . . . I think we can do better than that. We can have the Norman Rockwell image of a turkey on a platter, one that is great to eat. We just need a little help.

A whole turkey needs balance.

My solution is to go for balance. I cook a whole turkey to 155°F in the breast, plus five minutes. That little extra bit of doneness in the white meat gives the legs enough time to cook themselves to tenderness. Now, if you really are a dark meat fan, and don't care that Aunt Ethyl has to chew her white meat more, go ahead and get to 165°F in the breast—the dark meat will be terrific, even if the white meat is right on the edge of drying out. Or you can move on to the next section, where I pull out all my extra turkey tricks.

Again, safety first. Follow the USDA guideline of 165°F in the breast if you have guests who could be compromised. Better safe than sorry.

Better Turkey Through Science

Here are all the finesse techniques I use to get an evenly cooked turkey. These tricks even out the cooking, slow down the white meat, and speed up the dark meat, to get us where we want to be—juicy breast meat and tender dark meat. I list the techniques in order of importance; if you're in a hurry or don't feel like fussing, just go with the rotisserie and a brine and call it a day. If you're going all out, do everything on this list—your guests will be amazed, no matter their preference for white or dark meat.

Spin it to win it.

Our first solution is cooking with a rotisserie. (Hey—that's the whole point of this book!) The spinning bird creates convection currents in the grill, transferring more of the heat to the meat. Rotating the bird also evens out the heat, exposing part of the turkey to a blast of heat and then spinning it away. Both of these combine to cook the bird more evenly—the outside of the bird doesn't overcook while the inside comes up to temperature. This is important for the thick breast on a turkey—we want the inside to cook at about the same rate as the outside so we don't have a layer of dried-out meat around a juicy center.

Also, trussing the turkey helps the dark meat by pushing the drumsticks out away from the bird and exposing them to more heat. This cooks them a little quicker than the breast, which is exactly what we want.

We could be done here. Rotisserie cooking just does a better job than plain old roasting, especially for poultry. That's why cooks and chefs have made the extra effort to spit-roast for hundreds of years. But . . . these are modern times. We can do better.

Try the salt of the earth.

Brining has exploded in American home cooking over the past couple of decades. Turkey is a large part of that—a brined turkey is an extra moist turkey, with extra liquid trapped in the meat. We'll get into the details in the seasoning chapter, but you want to brine your turkey, especially if you are a white meat fan.

Ice is nice.

Next up is a trick I learned from Harold McGee, author of the bible of food science, On Food and Cooking. His insight: We want the breast to cook slower than the legs, right? Why not strap a couple of ice packs on there? I take the turkey out of the refrigerator an hour before cooking. I fill a gallon zip-top bag with a layer of ice, zip it closed, and rest the bag of ice on the turkey breast, making sure it doesn't touch the legs. I leave the bag of ice on the breast until right before the turkey goes in the grill, giving the legs have a head start.

Hold the feet to the fire.

Finally, here's a trick I learned from Jamie Purviance, the cookbook author for Weber grills. Instead of a traditional indirect fire with the coals banked to the sides of the grill, I make a U of fire on the side of the grill closer to the legs. This concentrates the heat on the tail end of the bird where the dark meat is, cooking it faster than the white meat. On my gas grill, I set up an indirect fire by lighting the burners on the leg side of the grill, not the breast side. (We'll talk about this more in the charcoal and gas grill setup chapters.)

How Long Is This Going to Take?

This is the part where every cookbook lies to you . . . um . . . I mean, the part where every cookbook has to estimate based on all the variables in your backyard. Grill running hot? In the hot sun? Cold and windy? Thick-breasted turkey? All of these affect cooking time.

That said, I estimate about 11 minutes per pound of bird. When I cook a 12- to 14-pound bird at a grill temperature of 350°F to an internal temperature of 155°F in the breast, it takes about 2 ½ hours.

Rotisserie Turkey Timing Table

Whole turkey, at 350°F...

Weight	Time
6 to 9 pounds	1½ to 2 hours
10 to 17 pounds	2 to 2 ½ hours
18 to 21 pounds	2 ½ to 3 hours
22 to 26 pounds	3 to 3 ½ hours
27 to 30 pounds	3 ½ to 4 hours

Turkey Breast Timing Table

Turkey Breast, at 350°F...

Weight	Time
6 pounds	75 minutes (1 ¼ hours)
7 pounds	90 minutes (1½ hours)
8 pounds	105 minutes (1 ¾ hours)

TRUSSING AND SPITTING

Trussing a Whole Turkey

Rotisserie turkey, with crackling skin and tender meat, is fantastic.
But the bird has to be trussed into a tight package and secured on the
rotisserie spit. There are wings, thighs, and drumsticks sticking out

everywhere, and they need to be locked down. Flopping wings and wobbly legs will pull the bird loose from the spit forks as it cooks and tenderizes.

A trussing trick is a double looping the first tie in the knot. The extra loop adds tension when you pull the string tight, holding tight while you finish the knot. Cross the string, loop it under once, then once more to add an extra loop.

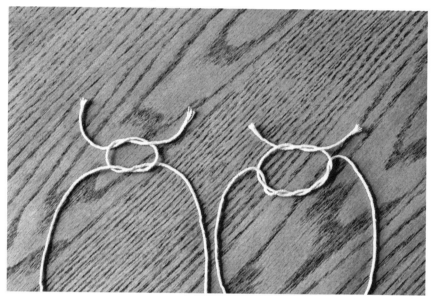

Cut a piece of butcher's twine four times the length of the bird. Fold the wingtips tightly under the bird; this locks them in place so they won't flop around. Set the bird on its backbone, with the drumsticks pointing at you and the breast and wings away from you. Find the middle of the piece of string, reach around to the front of the bird, and loop that middle over the nub of the neck. Wrap both sides of the string around the breast, just above the wing, bring them together at the cavity behind the bird, and pull them taut. Tie a knot at the opening of the cavity—remember, start the knot with a double loop— and pull the knot tight to plump up the breast.

Next, tie the drumsticks. Take the ends of the string in both hands, pull down between the knobs of the drumsticks, then loop out and up, catching the knobs of the drumsticks with the string. Pull the knobs of the drumsticks together by starting a knot; double loop above the drumsticks and pull tight. Keep tightening the knot and pushing on the knobs until they cross. Continue to tighten the knot and push the knobs toward the cavity until the drumsticks are up against the first knot. Finish off the knot and trim any extra string.

Spitting the Turkey

Tighten the first spit fork on the spit. Run the spit through the bird, starting at the cavity in the back, sinking the fork's tines into the thighs. Slide the second spit fork onto the spit and push it into the bird's breast meat, just above the wings. Keep pushing until the bird is squeezed between both forks. Make sure the bird is centered on the spit, then tighten the second fork to lock the bird in place. That's it—the bird is ready for the rotisserie.

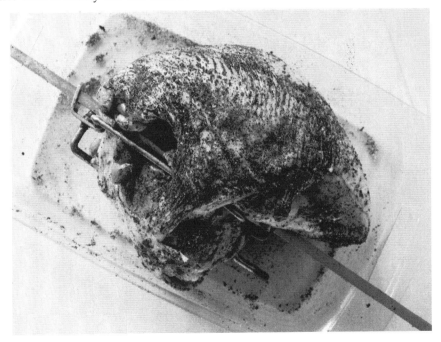

Trussing and Spitting a Turkey Breast

Looking for rotisserie with the least amount of effort? Try a turkey breast. No trussing is necessary; a turkey breast is already a compact piece of meat, held together by the ribcage and keel bone. The only tricky part is securing it on the spit—aim just above the wing joints and push the forks together tight.

To spit a turkey breast, attach one fork to the spit, a little offset from the center. Run the spit through the cavity in the back, and push the fork into the meat just above the wing joint. Slide the other fork onto the spit and push it until it meets the first fork—the two forks should overlap. Push the forks together, hard, then tighten down the second fork to hold the breast on the spit. That's it—the turkey breast is ready for the rotisserie.

GAS GRILL SETUP

Setup for a Whole Turkey

Set up your grill for cooking at indirect medium heat (325° to 350°F). Remove the grill grates and the covers over the burners in the middle of the grill to make sure there is clearance for the turkey to spin. Preheat the grill with the lid closed and all burners on high for 15 minutes. Turn off the burners on one side of the grill, leaving burners on the drumstick side of the grill lit, then adjust the burners to get an internal grill temperature of 325° to 350°F. Try to get all the heat on the drumsticks side of the grill.

For example, cooking a whole turkey on my six-burner grill, I leave the end burner and the one next to it on high, and make sure to skewer the turkey so the legs are pointing toward those lit burners. This concentrates the heat on the dark meat, which I want to cook more than the breast.

If your grill can't hold at least 325°F with only the burners on the drumstick side lit, go ahead and light a burner on the other side. Keep it as low as possible while still heating the grill to 350°F.)

Setup for a Turkey Breast

Because all we're cooking is white meat, we can use a traditional indirect medium heat setup for a turkey breast. Remove the grill grates for clearance. Preheat the grill with the lid closed and all burners on high for 15 minutes. Turn off the middle burners, leaving the outside burners on, and adjust the burners to get an internal grill temperature of 325° to 350°F. On my six-burner grill, for indirect medium heat I leave the two end burners on high, and turn off the middle four burners.

Displaying Adaptability

Every grill is different. Adjust your burners until you get the right temperature in your grill. The only hard-and-fast rule is indirect heat—make sure no burners under the drip pan are lit.

Gas Grills with Infrared Rotisserie Burners

Infrared rotisserie burners are a great invention. They make it possible for a very expensive gas grill to almost have the browning power of a charcoal grill. (Not quite, but almost.) Infrared burners help with short cooking times—an hour or less—but all the recipes in this book are for big birds, which take a lot longer. That makes using an infrared burner tricky. If the turkey has a spice rub on it, it's going to burn before a two-to-three-hour cook is done.

I use the infrared burner to simulate charcoal burn-down. I start the grill set up for medium heat, with my infrared burner also set to medium—this bumps the heat up to medium-high, about 425°F in my grill. Then I check the turkey every 30 minutes. Once it is well browned, I turn off the infrared burner and let the main burners do the rest of the cooking. This is even more of a "your mileage may vary" situation than a regular grill—infrared burners go from "helps a little with browning" to "hotter than the surface of the sun." If this is your first cook with an infrared burner, keep a close eye on things, checking every 15 minutes of so, and shut off the infrared burner once the turkey looks good and browned.

CHARCOAL GRILL SETUP

Whole Turkey: The U of Fire

Once again, for a whole turkey, we want to concentrate the heat on the legs and away from the breast.

Fill a charcoal chimney three-quarters full of charcoal, about 45 briquette, and light it. Wait for the coals to be mostly covered with gray ash. Pour the charcoal in a U shape on the drumstick side of the grill. Set the drip pan inside the U of charcoal.

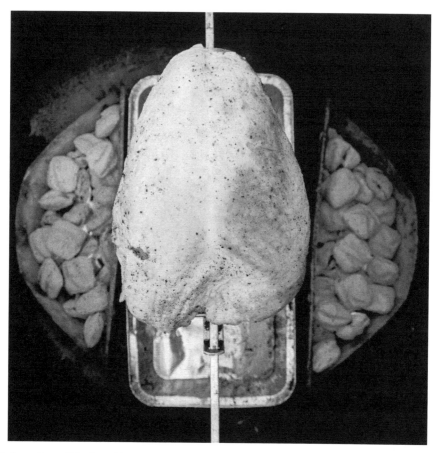

Setup for a Turkey Breast

Fill a charcoal chimney three-quarters full of charcoal, about 45 briquettes, and light it Wait for the coals to be mostly covered with gray ash. Pour the charcoal in two piles on the sides of the charcoal grate. Put the drip pan in the center of the grill, between the piles of charcoal. If your grill comes with charcoal baskets, use them. They are a big help in holding the coals in piles on the sides of the grill.

Charcoal Burn-Down and Heat Maintenance

A batch of charcoal briquettes will burn down in about an hour. This is a good thing at first—I start out with a blast of heat, browning the skin and rendering some fat, then finish with a lower fire. This brings the bird gently to its final cooking temperature.

The downside to charcoal burn-down is that eventually, all the coals burn out and I lose the heat. I need to keep the fire going for about two hours for a turkey breast, and about three hours for a whole turkey. To keep the fire going, I add 16 unlit charcoal briquettes to the grill every hour. I set them on the pile of lit coals in the grill, and close the lid; the existing fire catches the briquettes and keeps the heat going. The trick to this is to keep the lid open as little as possible, to keep the heat in the grill. I count out the coals into my charcoal chimney before I open the lid, so I can quickly dump them into the grill when the lid is open.

Charcoal: Briquettes or Lump?

I'm a briquette man — give me my good old blue bag of Kingsford. I don't have much luck with lump charcoal. Lump burns hotter and quicker — which means it's either too hot and charring the bird, or the coals have burnt out, the grill is cold, and I'm trying to light another chimney to save the turkey. Also, lump charcoal has a lot of variability among brands and even between bags — one bag may have a bunch of smaller pieces of charcoal, another may have lots of big chunks, a third may be mixed between the two.

Why use lump when it's more complicated? Because lump charcoal is pure wood, with no additives. Briquettes are mainly wood, but do have have other ingredients in there to act as binders and hold the briquette together. Some people say they can taste a difference, that natural lump charcoal burns cleaner than briquettes. I'm sure they're right, but if there is a difference in taste, I can't tell. If you want to use lump, you'll need to experiment — different types of lump charcoal have different sizes, which makes them highly variable. Start by cutting back on the initial amount of charcoal (down to half a chimney), and add extra lump charcoal to the fire every 45 minutes instead of every hour. Or split the difference and look for a brand of "all-natural" briquettes.

SEASONING THE BIRD

Seasoning the turkey can be as simple as sprinkling it with salt and pepper right before it goes on the grill. And that can be enough to make a good bird. But we can do better.

Smoking with Wood

There are many different ways to season a turkey, from wet and dry brines to rubs, pastes, and glazes. But first, we'll talk about the secret weapon of grilled turkey—flavoring a bird with wood smoke.

Differences for Gas and Charcoal Grills

Gas grills are at a disadvantage when it comes to smoking. When propane burns, one of the byproducts is combustion gases. Gas grills are vented to let those combustion gases escape. Unfortunately, that means any wood smoke is also vented before it has much time to work on the turkey. You'll always get better results smoking in a charcoal grill; it is more of a sealed environment. Also, the charcoal itself provides a little bit of smoke flavor.

Now, if you have a gas grill, don't give up; a little smoke flavor is better than none. Go ahead and use smoking wood in a gas grill.

Wood chunks in charcoal grills

Wood chunks are perfect for charcoal grills—drop one on the lit charcoal and you're good to go. I use one or two fist-size chunks of smoking wood for a turkey, depending on how much smoke flavor I want. More than that and I find it overwhelms the flavor of the turkey. If all you have is wood chips, they'll work, but they burn faster and don't make quite as much smoke. 2 cups of wood chips will replace two fist-sized chunks of smoking wood.

Chips in gas grills

Chunks of wood don't work in gas grills, so we turn to wood chips. There are three ways to use wood chips in a gas grill.

1.   Some high-end grills come with a dedicated smoker box and burner—if you have one, use it. Preheat the grill with the smoker burner on, then pour the chips in the smoker box right before the turkey goes on the grill.

2.   If the grill doesn't have a smoker box, you can buy a generic smoker box—usually steel or cast iron—and set it on the burner cover over one of your lit burners. Preheat the grill first, then add the

smoker box once the grill is hot. Added smoker boxes work well, and I recommend one if you don't have a dedicated smoker box.

3.   If you're in a pinch, you can use wood chips in an aluminum foil envelope. Put the chips on a sheet of heavy-duty foil in a tightly packed single layer, fold the foil over, and crimp the edges. Poke a few holes in the foil with a paring knife to let the smoke escape. Use this envelope like a smoker box; put it on the burner cover directly over one of your lit burners.

To soak or not to soak?

My thinking on soaking has evolved. I don't bother soaking wood any more. It doesn't seem to matter with wood chunks in a charcoal grill — the heat of the grill dries out the wood pretty quickly. I use wood chips on a gas grill, and there my problem is getting the smoker box hot enough to get the wood smoking. I don't want wet chips slowing down the smoking in a gas grill. So no soaking wood for me.

Seasoning Methods

Now let's talk about seasoning the bird itself. What does the bird need to taste good?

Salt and Pepper

As I said, sprinkling a turkey with salt and pepper right before it goes on the grill does a good job of seasoning. Combined with wood smoke, it makes an excellent turkey. But if you have time, you can do a better job of seasoning with a brine.

Brining

Wet brining is true brining. A brine is a saltwater solution, so wet brining — soaking a turkey in salty water — is really brining. "Dry brine" is a misnomer — no water, no brine. But enough semantics — on with the seasoning.

Dry brine

This is my favorite way to season a turkey. It is as simple as salting the bird; I just do it ahead of time. A dry brine works like a wet brine, denaturing protein and penetrating deep into the meat, but without the extra water of a wet brine. I prefer the way turkey tastes with a dry brine, especially the dark meat, but then I'm a dark meat fan—give me my drumstick and I'm happy. Dry brining does wonders for the taste of the breast as well, seasoning it through and giving it a meatier flavor, but it doesn't add the extra cushion from overcooking that a wet brine does. I keep a close eye on my turkey, get it off the grill right at 155°F, and enjoy the deeper turkey flavor.

To use a dry brine, rub the brine into the breast meat (under the skin), all over the turkey, and inside both the neck and body cavity. Cover with plastic wrap and refrigerate; remove the plastic wrap for the last 24 hours. If you are dry brining for 24 hours or less, skip the plastic wrap. If you are closer to cooking than four hours, dry brining won't help—wait until right before you truss the turkey to rub it with the salt and spices.

Wet brine

For most meats I prefer dry brines: I get the seasoning without the extra water. But with a turkey, this isn't a clear-cut decision. Wet brining plumps up the breast of the turkey, adding moisture to keep it from drying out and giving an extra cushion during cooking. Let the bird go to 165°F or (gasp) 170°F, and a brined turkey will have breast meat that's not completely dried out.

The other reason wet brining works for turkey is the long cooking time. Normally, wet brining makes poultry skin flabby and soft. The skin absorbs the water in the brine, and it takes too long to cook it out. But a turkey is in the grill for so long that the water cooks out with enough time left for the skin to crisp up.

Now, there is one big downside to wet brining: the amount of brine needed. A 14-pound turkey is huge, and you need a lot of brine to cover it. That means you need something big enough to submerge a turkey, and you need someplace cold to put it while it brines. I make this work with my huge 12-quart stockpot and my second refrigerator in the basement. The 12-quart pot is just barely large enough to submerge a 14-pound turkey—I fill it right up to the top, and the tips of the drumsticks are occasionally just above the waterline—and I empty out the downstairs fridge before Thanksgiving so I can slide the pot with the bird in there. And I do mean slide—a 14-pound bird submerged in 8 quarts of brine weighs *[does math . . . a pint's a pound, two pints to a quart]* 30 pounds, not counting the weight of the pot. Yikes. And move it carefully—you don't want to spill. (Not that I've ever slipped and dumped turkey-contaminated brine all over, dripping down into the crisper drawer and all over the floor. No, not me, it never happened.)

Injection Brine

Years ago I saw John Madden with a deep-fried Cajun turkey after the Thanksgiving football game. I had to try it! All the deep-fried turkey recipes injected a marinade, so I dutifully bought an injector kit, melted butter, stirred in the spices, and poked the bird all over. What I got was streaks of marinade and Cajun spices surrounded by dry, unseasoned meat. I quit injection marinades and deep-frying, and moved on to brined, grilled turkey.

This year, I'm going back . . . to the future. The Modernist Cuisine at Home cookbook convinced me to dust off my injector kit and injection-brine my turkey. Injection brining solves a number of turkey problems.

- **Injection brining penetrates deeper into the meat:** Unlike fat-based injection marinades, a saltwater brine is actually absorbed into the surrounding meat. No more streaks of seasoning—the meat is seasoned all the way through.

- **It's faster than wet or dry brining:** Injecting a brine deep into the bird speeds up the brining process—it doesn't have to work its way into the meat from the outside. You can brine your turkey the night before Thanksgiving instead of starting days in advance.

- **The skin stays dry:** Wet brines can lead to flabby skin. Injecting the brine into the meat leaves the skin dry, so it can crisp up and brown.

- **Cleanup is easier:** No lugging around a huge pot of brine, contaminated by raw turkey juices. You use two cups of brine, and after injecting almost all of the brine is inside the turkey. No mess, no fuss.

The downside? I get a little squeamish every time I open the injection kit—these are some serious-looking needles.

How does injected turkey taste? I'm torn. I love my dry-brined turkey. An injection brine is more neutral. But it adds moisture to the turkey breast, giving it an extra cushion before the white meat hits that "dry as dust" stage. Not a huge cushion, mind you—get it off the grill as close to 160°F as you can—but I don't mind the extra moisture, and my wife (who prefers white meat) said this may be my best turkey ever.

Enhanced Turkeys

Watch out for the words "enhanced with a x% solution" on the turkey's wrapper. "Enhanced" means the turkey was brined at the processing plant. You're paying for extra water, and you risk over salting if you then brine it yourself. Try to find a "natural" turkey— that is, just turkey, no added water or brine.

Rubs and Pastes

Rubs are my favorite way to season the outside of a turkey. There are two major types: dry rubs, made up entirely of dried herbs and spices, and wet pastes, mixtures that include wet ingredients like olive oil, garlic, and fresh herbs (as well as dried herbs and spices.)

Now, I'm describing these as if they are separate from brines, but there can be a lot of overlap. I make my dry rubs with salt and use them as dry brines; I add salt to my wet pastes, to give them a wet brine effect. The rub itself doesn't penetrate the meat the way salt does—unlike salt, flavor molecules are too big to fit between meat fibers—but the rub seasons the outside of the meat while the salt penetrates deep inside. The result is multiple layers of flavors—spices on the surface and salt all the way through.

Rubs and pastes are a quick way to add flavor if you don't have time to brine. You don't have to plan ahead.

One thing to watch out for with rubs and pastes: The ingredients burn quicker than the turkey itself. (Some recipes use this on purpose — think of Cajun blackened redfish, for example.) Charcoal burn-down helps avoid this in a charcoal grill; the temperature usually drops before the spices have a chance to burn. In a gas grill, check the turkey after a half an hour, and every 15 minutes after that; turn the heat down to 300°F, or turn off the infrared rotisserie burner, when the rub is nicely browned.

Glazes

Glazes are brushed on the turkey at the end of cooking to build another layer of flavor. Glazes usually have sugar in them — think sweet, sticky barbecue sauce — and sugar will burn, even in a low grill. I apply glazes in layers during the last 15 minutes of cooking, one layer every five minutes or so. This builds a thick crust of glaze on the bird but doesn't leave the glaze enough time to burn.

EQUIPMENT

Here is my list of recommended equipment for rotisserie grilling.

Rotisserie

You do need the rotisserie for your grill if you are going to rotisserie a turkey. It should include a spit, spit forks, a motor to turn the spit, and some sort of bracket to hold the motor and the spit. Some grills have the bracket built in; others have metal tabs that screw on the outside of the grill box to act as mounting points. My favorite is the rotisserie ring for my kettle grill. The ring sits between the grill's body and the lid, lifting the lid and giving me extra space to fit a large beast to roast. Like, say, a turkey.

Heatproof Gloves

Your rotisserie spit is branding-iron hot when it comes off the fire. (Trust me—I've been branded a few times.) Protect your hands with a set of welding gloves or grill gloves. Get a pair that is long enough to protect your wrists and forearms. I've been burned (ha) by oven mitts that only covered my hands—I'm not paying attention, shift my grip on the spit, and sear a line into my forearm, just above the mitt.

Trussing String

Heavy-duty trussing string is also called butcher's twine because it's what butchers use to tie roasts. Make sure it's a heavy grade of string—nothing is more frustrating than a string that snaps as you pull the legs tight. Also, watch out for string with nylon in it—nylon can melt in the heat of the grill, and you don't want a melted-nylon-flavored turkey. Watch out for colorful string, too—if it is any color other than white or off-tan, it is probably nylon.

Drip Pan

A drip pan keeps your grill clean and prevents grease fires. Disposable aluminum foil pans are quick and easy - crumple them up when you're done cooking, and throw them away. Look for pans that are 9 by 13-inches, but don't worry about the exact dimensions - a few inches in either direction won't hurt. I usually buy 10 by 12-inch half size steam table pans. They are inexpensive if you buy them in bulk at restaurant supply stores.

In the recipes, you'll see red and blue speckled pans as my drip pans. Those are Crow Canyon enameled steel large roasting pans, 11 by 13-inches, dedicated for use in my grill. I got tired of the waste (and expense) from throwing away aluminum foil pans, so I bought these. (OK, you got me. The main reason I bought them? They look better in pictures. I'm a food blogger; pretty pictures are in my blood.)

Instant-Read Thermometer

As you can tell from my turkey temperature rant, a thermometer is essential for a properly cooked turkey. I love my Thermapen—an expensive thermocouple probe thermometer, but I'm a fanatic. (If you too are a cooking fanatic, you don't need me to tell you about Thermapens. You probably own one already.) Look for a thermometer with a thin probe. Get an instant-read thermometer with a digital readout or an analog dial; old-school bulb thermometers, with their pencil-thick probes, are only worth using if you are desperate.

Spring-Loaded Kitchen Tongs

When I'm cooking, 12-inch spring loaded tongs are my hands. They have thousands of uses in the kitchen. For the rotisserie, they help me turn the hot spit fork screws and slide the turkey and forks off of the spit.

Kitchen Scissors or Shears

Kitchen scissors aren't absolutely necessary—you can get by with cutting your string using a knife—but it sure is easier to reach in there and snip the string loose with scissors.

Chef's Knife or Carving Set

After showing the turkey to your guests and waiting for the ooohs and aaahs to finish, you need to carve the meat off the bones. I've used everything from a paring knife (ugh) to fancy carving sets with matching forks and knives. The carving set was very nice, but most of the time I grab my trusty 8-inch chef's knife and start carving.

Carving Board with a Deep Juice Groove

A big bird needs a big carving board. Look for one that is at least 14 by 20-inches, with a deep groove around the outside to catch the turkey juices as you carve.

FAQ

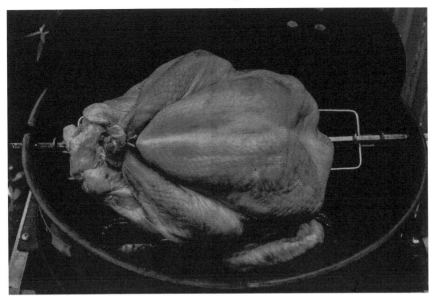

Q: How big of a bird can I fit on my rotisserie?
A: Bigger than you think.
A kettle grill, with its added rotisserie ring, can handle as big a bird as you've got; the rotisserie ring gives it extra clearance. A jumbo gas grill, one of the six-burner monster grills (like my beloved Weber Summit) can fit a 24-to-25-pound bird. Smaller grills start to run into problems with clearance between the turkey and the lid—for a regular-size grill, I'd stick to a 16-pound bird, though I have heard reports from readers about fitting 20-pound birds on Weber's Genesis models, which is my standard for "regular-size grill."

Q: How do I take the bird's temperature?
A: In the thickest part of the breast.
I run the probe into the meat about an inch to the side of the neck cavity, deep into the meat - two to three inches - as shown in the picture above.

Q: Should I soak my smoking wood?
A: No, not really.

A lot of recipes recommend soaking smoking wood in water for at least an hour before using it on the grill. The theory is, this results in more smoke - the wood smolders instead of catching on fire.

My take? Skip the soak. Soaking just delays the smoke. The wood doesn't smolder - it takes a while to dry out, then generates the same amount of smoke it would have anyhow.

Q: Should I stuff a rotisserie turkey?
A: No.
Remember the chapter about turkey science and white meat? Stuffing throws a wrench into the gears. If you stuff the turkey, you have to cook the stuffing in the center of the bird to 150°F, plus five minutes, to be sure salmonella is killed. The problem is, by the time the center of the stuffing reaches 150°F, the outside of the bird will be wildly overcooked. Don't stuff the turkey.

But...what if I love stuffing?
That's OK - so do I. But I cook it in its own pan, separately from the turkey. See Turkey Sides (Page 92) for some recipes.

Q: How do I carve a turkey?
A: Carefully.
If you have a favorite way of carving a turkey, go ahead and use it. Here is my preferred method.

- Cut the legs free from the body of the bird, and cut the drumsticks away from the thighs. Leave the drumsticks whole (my favorite part!) and slice the meat from the thighs in ½-inch slices for dark meat lovers.

- Peel one breast half from the bird by working a knife down the keel bone, following the inside of the ribcage, from the top of the bird down to the wing.

- Once the breast half is free of the bird, set it skin side up on the carving board and slice it crosswise. Repeat with the other breast half.

- Finally, cut each wing away from the carcass. Separate the drumette from the wing and the wing from the wingtip.

- Arrange all these pieces on a platter and serve.

Q: What do I do with the pop up thermometer that came in the turkey?
A: Get rid of it.
Those pop-up thermometers—they look like little plastic plugs, stuck in the breast of the turkey—are notoriously unreliable. Before you truss the bird, get it out of there. Gently pull and wiggle until it comes free, then throw it away.

Q: What's the deal with all these different turkeys? Natural? Heritage? Organic? What does it all mean?
A: Here's what you need to know about turkey types.
Hen Versus Tom: A hen is a female turkey; a tom is a male. What's the difference? Size. Smaller turkeys—up to about 16 pounds—are hens. Above 16 pounds is probably a tom. I prefer hens—12 to 14 pounds—because they're easier to cook evenly. The huge breast on a tom makes it hard to get the interior of the breast cooked to 155°F before the outer edges start to overcook, even with the advantages inherent in rotisserie grilling. So what do I do if I need to feed more people? If fire up my other grill and cook a second 12-to-14-pound bird.

Natural Versus Enhanced: "Enhanced" means brined. I prefer natural and season it myself.

Watch out for enhanced turkeys—look for the words "enhanced with [a] x% solution" on the label. That means the turkey was brined at the factory. If the turkey is "enhanced with a natural solution" of more than 6 percent, it already has enough salt inside it. Cut the salt in the dry brine down to 1 tablespoon.

If at all possible, get a natural turkey. Sure, that enhanced turkey going for 59 cents a pound at the grocery store looks like a deal, but I'd rather pay extra for the natural turkey and do my own brining.

Kosher: Kosher is also a brined bird, because the koshering process involves salting. The koshering process is closer to a dry brine, though, so I prefer the results to enhanced birds.

Heritage: What we think of as a turkey is the Broad Breasted White breed—it's what you will find in your local grocery store. Heritage breeds are less common, and you'll have to seek out a Bourbon Red, Standard Bronze, Narragansett, or other breed of turkey if you're interested. Be ready to pay more—heritage breeds are much more expensive; don't expect a 59 cent special on these birds. They have a stronger turkey flavor than the traditional bird, and less white meat. I have heard mixed reports about them—some people love the extra flavor, some don't—so be careful about cooking one for Thanksgiving if you have never tried it. (I've cooked heritage birds a few times, and no one other than me noticed any differences.)

Organic, Free Range: Organic turkeys are regulated by the United States Department of Agriculture; certified organic turkey must eat organic feed, never receive antibiotics, and be free range. "Free range" is another USDA-regulated term, meaning the birds have access to the outdoors. ("Outdoors" can be anything from living on a grass pasture to having a small, fenced-in concrete pad outside the turkey house, so this term doesn't mean as much as it could. But at least the bird might see daylight.)

Pasture-Raised: The USDA does not regulate this term. The turkey actually lives on a pasture and feeds by foraging in the grass. (Free-range and organic birds usually eat turkey feed.) Generally, farmers call their turkeys "pasture raised" because they don't think free-range standards go far enough for bird welfare. If pasture-raised turkey interests you, get to know your farmer so you know their definition of "pasture raised" matches yours—the USDA is not watching to make sure they follow any rules.

Fresh versus Frozen: Fresh means never frozen. If you need to season the bird right away, find a fresh bird.

Frozen birds need to be thawed before cooking. The best way to do this is in the refrigerator, in a rimmed baking sheet or roasting pan. Plan ahead—it takes about a day per four pounds of bird, so a 12-pound turkey needs to start thawing three days ahead of time.

If you're in a hurry, you can use the cold water method of thawing. Make sure the turkey is wrapped in its original packaging, without any holes in the plastic. Submerge the turkey in cold water, changing the water every 30 minutes. It will take about 30 minutes per pound for the cold water thaw, so about six hours for a 12-pound bird.

Q: What do I do with the neck, back and giblets?
A: Remove before cooking—and save for turkey broth.
Don't forget to check both cavities of the bird—the front and inner cavities. The bird usually has a bag with the giblets in the front cavity, where the neck was, and the neck itself is stuffed in the central cavity of the bird. Remove them all and use them to make Giblet Gravy (Page 94) or Turkey Broth (Page 115).

Q: Can I use the pan drippings from a rotisserie turkey?
A: It depends. Are you cooking with charcoal or gas?
If you are using a charcoal grill, you're going to get ash in your drip pan. I don't think ashes make for good gravy, so I don't use the drippings. If you are using a gas grill, then maybe the drippings will be useable. Half the time the drippings burn too much; if you really want to use the drippings, add a cup of water to the drip pan to keep them from burning. Personally, I save the drip pan for potatoes or squash, and use the neck and giblets to in Giblet Gravy (Page 94).

Q: What if I don't have a rotisserie?
A: No rotisserie? No worries. Grilled turkey is fantastic.
Set up your grill as described in Gas Grill Setup (Page 19) or Charcoal Grill Setup (Page 21), with a drip pan in the middle and the heat on the sides. Instead of the rotisserie rig, put the grill grate back on the grill and set the bird on the grate directly over the drip pan. Cook a smaller turkey—14 pounds max—unless you are sure there is enough lid clearance in your grill for a bigger bird.

(And I'm impressed you bought this book, even though you don't have a rotisserie. Mom, is that you?)

RECIPES

WHOLE TURKEY RECIPES

Here are my recipes for the big bird. Most of my (good-looking, intelligent, kind-hearted) readers will check this chapter on Thanksgiving, then put the book away until next year. Please don't think of turkey as a once-a-year event. A whole turkey will feed a crowd, no matter when you need it; don't restrict it to the fourth week of November.

SIMPLE DRY-BRINED TURKEY

Here is a simple rotisserie turkey with a straightforward, basic dry brine: salt, brown sugar, and black pepper. Now, simple doesn't mean plain—dry brining adds a lot of flavor to the bird. Next, I add all the tricks I know—icing the breast, making the U of fire or lighting only the burners near the legs, adding a hint of wood smoke, and cooking to 155°F. This should balance the juiciness of the white meat with thoroughly cooking the dark meat. The end result? A great, simple turkey.

If you don't have the time to dry brine, rub the turkey with the dry brine right before you put it on the grill. It won't be as thoroughly seasoned, but it will be a great bird.

Equipment

Gallon-size zip-top plastic bag full of ice

2 fist-size chunks of smoking wood or 2 cups wood chips (hickory, oak, pecan, or a fruit wood; I love oak wine barrel staves)

Ingredients

Basic Dry Brine

¼ cup Diamond Crystal kosher salt or 3 tablespoons Morton's kosher salt (1½ ounces)
1 teaspoon light or dark brown sugar
½ teaspoon freshly ground black pepper

12-to-14-pound turkey

Directions

1. Dry-brine the turkey: One to 3 days before it is time to cook, mix the salt, sugar, and pepper in a small bowl. Gently work your fingers between the skin and the breast, then rub some of the brine directly onto the breast meat. Sprinkle and rub the rest of the dry brine evenly over the turkey. Make sure to season the neck and back cavity of the turkey, too. Put the turkey on a rack over a roasting pan or rimmed baking sheet and cover with plastic wrap. If you are dry brining for only 24 hours, skip the plastic wrap. Refrigerate.

Remove the plastic wrap the night before cooking to allow the skin to dry.

If you are closer than 4 hours to cooking, just rub the turkey with the brine right before you truss it.

2. Truss and spit the turkey: One hour before cooking, remove the turkey from the refrigerator. Fold the wingtips underneath the bird, then truss the turkey. Skewer the turkey on the rotisserie spit, securing it with the spit forks. To keep the breast meat cool, set the bag of ice on the turkey's breast, arranging it so the ice does not touch the thighs or drumsticks. Let the turkey rest at room temperature until it is time to cook.

3. Set up the grill: Set up the grill for indirect medium heat (325° to 350°F), with the drip pan in the middle of the grill and the heat concentrated on the drumstick side of the grill. Use the U of charcoal or turn on burners on one side of the grill, if possible (see the Charcoal Grill Setup and Gas Grill Setup chapters for more details). Add the smoking wood to the fire.

4. Rotisserie the turkey: Discard the bag of ice. Put the spit on the grill with the drumsticks pointed toward the heat. Start the rotisserie spinning, and make sure the drip pan is centered under the turkey. Close the lid. If you are using a charcoal grill, add 16 unlit briquettes every hour to keep the heat going. Cook until the turkey reaches 155°F in the thickest part of the breast, about 2 ½ hours.

5. Carve and serve: Remove the turkey from the grill, remove the spit from the turkey, and cut the trussing string loose. Let the turkey rest for 15 to 30 minutes before carving. Arrange the carved turkey on a platter and serve.

TURKEY DRY-BRINED WITH LEMON AND HERBS

Time for a more complex dry brine, with layers of flavors. Lemon zest and herbs flavor the outside of the turkey while the salt does its brining magic and penetrates deep into the meat.

I like fruitwood with this rub—the lighter smoke flavor from apple or cherry wood goes well with the citrus of the lemon zest.

Equipment

Gallon-size zip-top plastic bag full of ice

2 fist-size chunks of smoking wood or 2 cups wood chips (hickory, oak, pecan, or a fruit wood; I love oak wine barrel staves)

Ingredients

Lemon-Herb Dry Brine

¼ cup Diamond Crystal kosher salt or 3 tablespoons Morton's kosher salt (1½ ounces)

2 lemons, zest grated, lemons halved

2 cloves garlic, grated

2 teaspoons fresh rosemary leaves, minced

2 teaspoons fresh thyme leaves, minced

½ teaspoon freshly ground black pepper

¼ teaspoon red pepper flakes

12-to-14-pound turkey

Directions

1. Dry-brine the turkey: One to 3 days before it is time to cook, mix the salt, lemon zest, garlic, rosemary, thyme, black pepper, and red pepper flakes in a small bowl. Gently work your fingers between the skin and the breast, then rub some of the brine directly onto the breast meat. Sprinkle and rub the rest of the dry brine evenly over the turkey. Make sure to season the neck and back cavity of the turkey, too. Stuff the lemon halves into the back cavity. Put the turkey on a rack over a roasting pan or rimmed baking sheet and cover with plastic wrap. If you are only dry brining for 24 hours, skip the plastic wrap. Refrigerate.

Remove the plastic wrap the night before cooking to allow the skin to dry.

If you are closer than 4 hours to cooking, just rub the turkey with the brine right before you truss it.

2. Truss and spit the turkey: One hour before cooking, remove the turkey from the refrigerator. Fold the wingtips underneath the bird, then truss the turkey. Skewer the turkey on the rotisserie spit, securing it with the spit forks. To keep the breast meat cool, set the bag of ice on the turkey's breast, arranging it so the ice does not touch the thighs or drumsticks. Let the turkey rest at room temperature until it is time to cook.

3. Set up the grill: Set up the grill for indirect medium heat (325° to 350°F), with the drip pan in the middle of the grill and the heat concentrated on the drumstick side of the grill. Use the U of charcoal or turn on burners on one side of the grill, if possible (see the Charcoal Grill Setup and Gas Grill Setup chapters for more details). Add the smoking wood to the fire.

4. Rotisserie the turkey: Discard the bag of ice. Put the spit on the grill with the drumsticks pointed toward the heat. Start the rotisserie spinning, and make sure the drip pan is centered under the turkey. Close the lid. If you are using a charcoal grill, add 16 unlit briquettes every hour to keep the heat going. Cook until the turkey reaches 155°F in the thickest part of the breast, about 2 ½ hours.

5. Carve and serve: Remove the turkey from the grill, remove the spit from the turkey, and cut the trussing string loose. Let the turkey rest for 15 to 30 minutes before carving. (Leave the lemon halves in the bird - they gave their flavor up while cooking.) Arrange the carved turkey on a platter and serve.

Turkey Dry-Brined With Sage and Lemon

Thanksgiving smells like sage. I use it in my stuffing and, when I'm feeling traditional, to season my turkey. Here's a dry brine based on the most traditional of Thanksgiving herbs.

Equipment

Gallon-size zip-top plastic bag full of ice

2 fist-size chunks of smoking wood or 2 cups wood chips (hickory, oak, pecan, or a fruit wood; I love oak wine barrel staves)

Ingredients

Sage-Lemon Dry Brine

¼ cup Diamond Crystal kosher salt or 3 tablespoons Morton's kosher salt (1½ ounces)

2 lemons, zest grated, lemons halved

½ teaspoon ground sage

½ teaspoon dried thyme

½ teaspoon freshly ground black pepper

12-to-14-pound turkey

Directions

1. Dry-brine the turkey: One to 3 days before it is time to cook, mix the salt, lemon zest, sage, thyme, and pepper in a small bowl. Gently work your fingers between the skin and the breast, then rub some of the brine directly onto the breast meat. Sprinkle and rub the rest of the dry brine evenly over the turkey. Make sure to season the neck and back cavity of the turkey, too. Stuff the lemon halves in the back cavity of the bird. Put the turkey on a rack over a roasting pan or rimmed baking sheet and cover with plastic wrap. If you are only dry brining for 24 hours, skip the plastic wrap. Refrigerate.

Remove the plastic wrap the night before cooking to allow the skin to dry.

If you are closer than 4 hours to cooking, just rub the turkey with the brine right before you truss the it

2. Truss and spit the turkey: One hour before cooking, remove the turkey from the refrigerator. Fold the wingtips underneath the bird, then truss the turkey. Skewer the turkey on the rotisserie spit, securing it with the spit forks. To keep the breast meat cool, set the bag of ice on the turkey's breast, arranging it so the ice does not touch the thighs or drumsticks. Let the turkey rest at room temperature until it is time to cook.

3. Set up the grill: Set up the grill for indirect medium heat (325° to 350°F), with the drip pan in the middle of the grill and the heat concentrated on the drumstick side of the grill. Use the U of charcoal or turn on burners on one side of the grill, if possible (see the Charcoal

Grill Setup and Gas Grill Setup chapters for more details). Add the smoking wood to the fire.

4. Rotisserie the turkey: Discard the bag of ice. Put the spit on the grill with the drumsticks pointed toward the heat. Start the rotisserie spinning, and make sure the drip pan is centered under the turkey. Close the lid. If you are using a charcoal grill, add 16 unlit briquettes every hour to keep the heat going. Cook until the turkey reaches 155°F in the thickest part of the breast, about 2 ½ hours.

5. Carve and serve: Remove the turkey from the grill, remove the spit from the turkey, and cut the trussing string loose. Let the turkey rest for 15 to 30 minutes before carving. (Leave the lemon halves in the bird - they gave their flavor up while cooking.) Arrange the carved turkey on a platter and serve.

Turkey with Basic Wet Brine

This recipe takes me back. In the late 1990s—let's say 1999—I learned about brining from Cooks Illustrated and Alton Brown. That lead to a string of great turkeys on the grill. As the 2000s progressed, I learned about dry brining from Judy Rodgers, and started playing around with my rotisserie. I drifted away from wet brines.

That doesn't mean there's anything wrong with this recipe. It still turns out a delicious turkey, one I was proud to serve for years. If you're looking for juicy breast meat, a wet brine is the way to go. Or let's say you get wrapped up in the football games on Thanksgiving— a wet brine leaves you some extra wiggle room before the turkey dries out.

Equipment

A container large enough to hold the turkey—I use my 12-quart stockpot

Gallon-size zip-top plastic bag full of ice

2 fist-size chunks of smoking wood or 2 cups wood chips (hickory, oak, pecan, or a fruit wood; I love oak wine barrel staves)

Ingredients

Brine

2 gallons cold water

½ cup table salt or 1 cup Diamond Crystal kosher salt (6 ounces)

¼ cup sugar

12-to-14-pound turkey

Instructions

1. Wet brine the turkey: Nine hours to one day before it is time to cook, pour the water into the container. Add the salt and sugar and stir until the salt and sugar dissolve. Submerge the turkey in the brine and refrigerate overnight. If you're pressed for time, brine for at least 8 hours; but don't go much longer than 24 hours.

2. Drain, truss, and spit the turkey: One hour before cooking, remove the turkey from the brine, let it drain, then pat dry with paper towels, inside and out. Discard the brine. Fold the wingtips underneath the bird, then truss the turkey. Skewer the turkey on the rotisserie spit, securing it with the spit forks. To keep the breast meat cool, set the bag of ice on the turkey's breast, arranging it so the ice does not touch the thighs or drumsticks. Let the turkey rest at room temperature until it is time to cook.

3. Set up the grill: Set up the grill for indirect medium heat (325° to 350°F), with the drip pan in the middle of the grill and the heat concentrated on the drumstick side of the grill. Use the U of charcoal or turn on burners on one side of the grill, if possible (see the Charcoal Grill Setup and Gas Grill Setup chapters for more details). Add the smoking wood to the fire.

4. Rotisserie the turkey: Discard the bag of ice. Put the spit on the grill with the drumsticks pointed toward the heat. Start the rotisserie spinning, and make sure the drip pan is centered under the turkey. Close the lid. If you are using a charcoal grill, add 16 unlit briquettes every hour to keep the heat going. Cook until the turkey reaches 155°F in the thickest part of the breast, about 2 ½ hours.

5. Carve and serve: Remove the turkey from the grill, remove the spit from the turkey, and cut the trussing string loose. Let the turkey rest for 15 to 30 minutes before carving. Arrange the carved turkey on a platter and serve.

Wet-Brined Turkey Stuffed With Herbs

This recipe is inspired by Rick Bayless, using just a hint of Mexican flavors to give it a south-of-the-border feel. After brining the turkey, I stuff the back cavity with herbs and aromatics to perfume the bird. Then I use mesquite, a controversial smoking wood. That's right—wood can be controversial. Want to start an Internet war? Mention mesquite in a barbecue forum. Oh, the rage! Mesquite has a very strong flavor—used in large quantities, it can overpower food. I use only a little here to give the turkey a distinct Southwestern flavor, not so much as to overwhelm it. If you're anti-mesquite, substitute oak or pecan, two other common Southwestern smoking woods.

Equipment

A container large enough to hold the turkey—I use my 12-quart stockpot

Gallon-size zip-top plastic bag full of ice

2 fist-size chunks of mesquite smoking wood or 2 cups wood chips (or substitute oak or pecan)

Ingredients

Brined Turkey

2 gallons cold water

½ cup table salt or 1 cup kosher salt (6 ounces)

¼ cup light or dark brown sugar

1 tablespoon crushed red pepper flakes

12-to-14-pound turkey

Cavity Stuffing

6 cloves garlic, peeled and crushed

1 bunch fresh marjoram

1 bunch fresh thyme

10 bay leaves

Directions

1. Wet-brine the turkey: Nine hours to one day before it is time to cook, pour the water into the container. Add the salt, sugar, and red pepper flakes and stir until the salt and sugar dissolve. Submerge the turkey in the brine and refrigerate overnight. If you're pressed for time, brine for at least 8 hours; don't go much longer than 24 hours.

2. Drain, stuff, truss, and spit the turkey: One hour before cooking, remove the turkey from the brine, let it drain, then pat dry with paper towels, inside and out. Discard the brine. Grab the garlic, herbs, and bay leaves in a loose handful and rub them all around the inside of the back cavity. Leave them in the back cavity to perfume the bird while it cooks.

Fold the wingtips underneath the bird, then truss the turkey. Skewer the turkey on the rotisserie spit, securing it with the spit forks. To keep the breast meat cool, set the bag of ice on the turkey's breast, arranging it so the ice does not touch the thighs or drumsticks. Let the turkey rest at room temperature until it is time to cook.

3. Set up the grill: Set up the grill for indirect medium heat (325° to 350°F), with the drip pan in the middle of the grill and the heat concentrated on the drumstick side of the grill. Use the U of charcoal or turn on burners on one side of the grill, if possible (see the Charcoal Grill Setup and Gas Grill Setup chapters for more details). Add the smoking wood to the fire.

4. Rotisserie the turkey: Discard the bag of ice. Put the spit on the grill with the drumsticks pointed toward the heat. Start the rotisserie spinning, and make sure the drip pan is centered under the turkey. Close the lid. If you are using a charcoal grill, add 16 unlit briquettes every hour to keep the heat going. Cook until the turkey reaches 155°F in the thickest part of the breast, about 2 ½ hours.

5. Carve and serve: Remove the turkey from the grill, remove the spit from the turkey, and cut the trussing string loose. Let the turkey rest for 15 to 30 minutes before carving. (Leave the garlic and herbs in the cavity - they gave their flavor up while cooking.) Arrange the carved turkey on a platter and serve.

INJECTION-BRINED TURKEY

Now it's time for a little mad (food) science. Bwahahahaha! *(I've always wanted an evil laugh. Instead, I sound like I need to clear my throat.)*

This recipe is inspired by Modernist Cuisine at Home, the slimmed-down version of the massive research encyclopedia by Nathan Myhrvold and Maxime Bilet. They cover all sorts of modern food techniques—sous vide, pressure cooking, flavored foams—but for turkey, injection brining is the obvious technique. It has all of the advantages of wet brining, plumping up the breast meat and making it juicy, without the mess and potentially flabby skin.

I'm also borrowing another technique of theirs and brushing the skin with a soy sauce and paprika glaze. This seasons the skin (which we're avoiding with the injection brine), and the protein in the soy sauce helps the skin brown.

Equipment

Marinade injector

Gallon-size zip-top plastic bag full of ice

Ingredients

Injection-Brined Turkey

2 cups water

2 tablespoons Diamond Crystal kosher salt or 1 tablespoon table salt (¾ ounces)

1 tablespoon sugar

12-to-14-pound turkey

Soy Sauce Glaze

2 tablespoons soy sauce

1 teaspoon smoked Spanish paprika or sweet paprika

Directions

1: Injection-brine the turkey: Nine hours to one day before it is time to cook, stir the water, salt, and sugar in a measuring cup until the salt and sugar dissolve. Fill the injector with brine. Inject the brine into the turkey, pushing the needle all the way in, then slowly pulling the needle out while depressing the plunger. Try to inject brine into the meat every 1 to 1 ½ inches in a repeating pattern, refilling the injector as needed. (This makes more brine than needed to inject in the turkey. Injection needles can't pull the last bit of brine out of a cup into the syringe, so I make extra.)

Start with the breast: Working at the front of the bird through the neck cavity, make three or four evenly spaced injections on each side. Inject brine into the wings, in the knobs of the drumettes (where the wings meet the breast) and between the two bones in the wing, going in the long way if you can. Move to the back of the bird and inject the thighs through the back cavity; each thigh should take two or three injections. Finally, inject the drumsticks with two injections, one in the knob of meat above the bone, one in the knob of meat below the bone.

2. Glaze the turkey: Mix the soy sauce and paprika and brush over the whole bird. Set the bird on a rack over a roasting pan or rimmed baking sheet and refrigerate, uncovered, at least 8 hours but not more than 24 hours.

3. Truss and spit the turkey: One hour before cooking, remove the turkey from the refrigerator. Fold the wingtips underneath the bird, then truss the turkey. Skewer the turkey on the rotisserie spit, securing it with the spit forks. To keep the breast meat cool, set the bag of ice on the turkey's breast, arranging it so the ice does not touch the thighs or drumsticks. Let the turkey rest at room temperature until it is time to cook.

4. Set up the grill: Set up the grill for indirect medium heat (325° to 350°F), with the drip pan in the middle of the grill and the heat concentrated on the drumstick side of the grill. Use the U of charcoal or turn on burners on one side of the grill, if possible (see the Charcoal Grill Setup and Gas Grill Setup chapters for more details).

5. Rotisserie the turkey: Discard the bag of ice. Put the spit on the grill with the drumsticks pointed toward the heat. Start the rotisserie spinning, and make sure the drip pan is centered under the turkey. Close the lid. If you are using a charcoal grill, add 16 unlit briquettes every hour to keep the heat going. Cook until the turkey reaches 155°F in the thickest part of the breast, about 2 ½ hours.

6. Carve and serve: Remove the turkey from the grill, remove the spit from the turkey, and cut the trussing string loose. Let the turkey rest for 15 to 30 minutes before carving. Arrange the carved turkey on a platter and serve.

Turkey Wrapped With Bacon

Everything tastes better with bacon, right?

An interviewer asked Christopher Kimball, founder and editor of Cooks Illustrated, about his favorite turkey. His answer? Turkey barded with bacon. The moment I heard that, I knew what I was cooking for Thanksgiving.

What does bacon do for a turkey? Rendered bacon fat will baste the lean breast meat while the turkey cooks, keeping it moist. Bacon adds a hint of salty, smoky flavor, which is nice, especially if you are cooking on a gas grill. And a layer of crisped bacon on the skin adds extra flavor to the relatively bland white meat. I also think the extra layer of bacon slows down the cooking of the breast, giving the drumsticks need extra time to cook.

So if you want to improve a traditional turkey, strap on some bacon.

Equipment

Gallon-size zip-top plastic bag full of ice

Ingredients

¼ cup Diamond Crystal kosher salt or 3 tablespoons Morton's kosher salt (1½ ounces)

½ teaspoon freshly ground black pepper

12-to-14-pound turkey

6 strips hickory-smoked bacon, regular sliced

Directions

1: Dry-brine the turkey: One to 3 days before it is time to cook, mix the salt and pepper in a small bowl. Gently work your fingers between the skin and the breast, then rub some of the brine directly onto the breast meat. Sprinkle and rub the rest of the dry brine evenly over the turkey. Make sure to season inside the neck and back cavity of the turkey, too. Put the turkey on a rack over a roasting pan or rimmed baking sheet and cover with plastic wrap. (If you are only dry brining for 24 hours, skip the plastic wrap.) Refrigerate.

Remove the plastic wrap the night before cooking to allow the skin to dry.

If you are closer than 4 hours to cooking, just rub the turkey with the brine right before you truss it.

2. Truss and spit the turkey: One hour before cooking, remove the turkey from the refrigerator. Fold the wingtips underneath the bird, then truss the turkey. Skewer the turkey on the rotisserie spit, securing it with the spit forks. Let the turkey rest at room temperature until it is almost time to cook. To keep the breast meat cool, set the bag of ice on the turkey's breast, arranging it so the ice does not touch the thighs or drumsticks.

3. Set up the grill: Set up the grill for indirect medium heat (325° to 350°F), with the drip pan in the middle of the grill and the heat concentrated on the drumstick side of the grill. Use the U of charcoal or turn on burners on one side of the grill, if possible (see the Charcoal Grill Setup and Gas Grill Setup chapters for more details).

4. Wrap the breast with bacon: Discard the bag of ice. Lay the bacon over the turkey breast, as shown in the picture above. Tie the bacon down onto the turkey: Loop a length of string under the turkey and behind the wings, then around the front of the breast to tie down the edge of the bacon strips near the turkey neck. Next, loop a length of string under the turkey, around the drumsticks, and over the top of the breast to tie down the other edge of the bacon strips. Finally, tie a third loop of string around the middle of the turkey to hold the bacon down in the middle. Make sure to tie the string tight at the edges, or the bacon will work loose as the turkey rotates.

5. Rotisserie the turkey: Put the spit on the grill with the drumsticks pointed toward the heat. Start the rotisserie spinning, and make sure the drip pan is centered under the turkey. Close the lid. If you are using a charcoal grill, add 16 unlit briquettes every hour to keep the heat going. Cook until the turkey reaches 155°F in the thickest part of the breast, about 2 ½ hours.

6. Carve and serve: Remove the turkey from the grill, remove the spit from the turkey, and cut all the strings loose. If some of the bacon peels away while you do this, use it as a chef's snack to reward yourself for all the hard work you're doing. Let the turkey rest for 15 to 30 minutes before carving. Carve the breast into crosswise slices so every piece has some of the skin with bacon attached. Arrange the carved turkey on a platter and serve

BBQ TURKEY

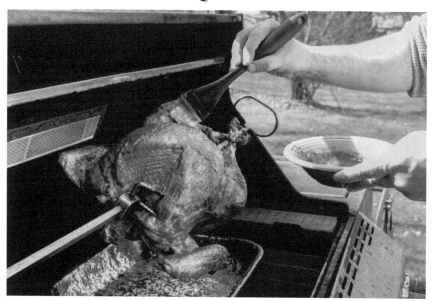

Now I'm crossing the streams. I'm taking the flavors of backyard barbecued chicken—a dry spice rub, sticky and sweet barbecue sauce, wood smoke—and using them to flavor turkey. If you think they work well on chicken, you should taste what happens when you use them with the big bird.

Of course, for barbecue we need hickory smoke. You could use the barbecue rub as a dry brine and sprinkle it on a day or two ahead of time—but I'm going straight for the grill on this one. Between the flavors of the wood smoke, the rub, and the barbecue sauce, I don't need the extra seasoning from a brine.

Equipment

Gallon-size zip-top plastic bag full of ice

2 fist-size chunks of hickory or 2 cups hickory chips

Ingredients

Barbecue Rub

3 tablespoons Diamond Crystal kosher salt or 2 tablespoons Morton's kosher salt (1 ounce)

2 tablespoons sweet paprika

2 teaspoons light or dark brown sugar

2 teaspoons chili powder

2 teaspoons garlic powder

2 teaspoons onion powder

½ teaspoon cayenne pepper

12-to-14-pound turkey

Barbecue Sauce

2 cups ketchup

½ cup light or dark brown sugar

½ cup molasses

½ cup cider vinegar

2 teaspoons Barbecue Rub (above)

Directions

1. Season the turkey: Mix the salt, paprika, sugar, chili powder, garlic powder, onion powder, and cayenne in a small bowl. Reserve 2 teaspoons of the rub for the barbecue sauce. Gently work your fingers between the skin and the breast, then rub some of the barbecue rub directly onto the breast meat. Sprinkle the turkey with the rest of the rub, inside and out, patting it onto the turkey to help it stick.

2. Truss and spit the turkey: Fold the wingtips under the bird and truss the turkey. Skewer the turkey on the rotisserie spit, securing it with the spit forks. To keep the breast meat cool, set the bag of ice on the turkey's breast, arranging it so the ice does not touch the thighs or drumsticks. Let the turkey rest at room temperature until the grill is ready.

3. Make the barbecue sauce: Whisk the ketchup, sugar, molasses, vinegar, and the reserved barbecue rub in a saucepan. Bring the sauce to a simmer over medium heat and simmer for 5 minutes, stirring often. Remove the sauce from the heat.

4. Set up the grill: Set up the grill for indirect medium heat (325° to 350°F), with the drip pan in the middle of the grill and the heat concentrated on the drumstick side of the grill. Use the U of charcoal or turn on burners on one side of the grill, if possible (see the Charcoal Grill Setup and Gas Grill Setup chapters for more details).

5. Rotisserie the turkey: Discard the bag of ice. Put the spit on the grill with the drumsticks pointed toward the heat. Start the rotisserie spinning, and make sure the drip pan is centered under the turkey. Close the lid. If you are using a charcoal grill, add 16 unlit briquettes every hour to keep the heat going. After 2 hours and 10 minutes of cooking, brush the turkey with a layer of barbecue sauce, then brush every 5 minutes for the next 20 minutes. Cook until the turkey reaches 155°F in the thickest part of the breast, about 2 ½ hours.

5. Carve and serve: Remove the turkey from the grill, remove the spit from the turkey, and cut the trussing string loose. Brush with one last coat of sauce, then let the turkey rest for 15 to 30 minutes before carving. Arrange the carved turkey on a platter and serve, passing the rest of the barbecue sauce at the table.

TURKEY BREAST (AND LEG) RECIPES

My mom always cooks an extra turkey breast on Thanksgiving. Actually, my mom cooks multiple whole turkeys and an extra turkey breast. My extended family shows up at my parents—and brings friends—so she often has more than 30 people at the table. Now, Mom never wants anyone to go away hungry or without a care package of leftovers, so she always errs on the side of more turkey.

The rest of the year, a turkey breast is a reasonably sized roast for a smaller group. I use turkey breast for Sunday dinner—it serves my family of five with a little left over for sandwiches in the week.

If you like the looks of a whole turkey recipe, cut the seasonings in half and use them on a turkey breast. Except for recipes where I stuff something in the back cavity, like herbs or a lemon half —the cavity on a turkey breast is wide open and everything falls out.

BASIC TURKEY BREAST

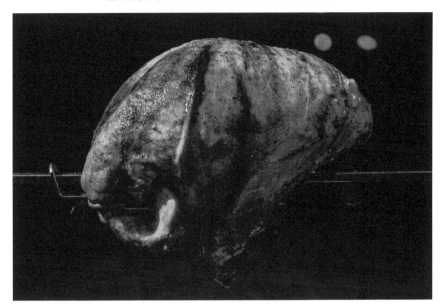

To go with turkey breast being the easiest thing to cook on the rotisserie, here's my simplest recipe—a salt-only dry brine for the turkey. Now, as I said before, simple doesn't mean plain—it's amazing how good a well-cooked turkey breast tastes with nothing but a little salt.

Ingredients

6-to-8-pound turkey breast

4 teaspoons Diamond Crystal kosher salt or 1 tablespoon Morton's kosher salt (½ ounce)

Directions

1. Dry-brine the turkey breast: Eight hours to 1 day before it is time to cook, pat the turkey breast dry with paper towels. Cut the extra skin away from the neck. Check inside the neck cavity and discard any big pieces of fat. Gently work the skin loose from the turkey breast, starting from the back of the bird, and rub 1 teaspoon of the salt directly on the breast meat. Pull the skin back into place, then sprinkle the rest of the salt all over the turkey breast, inside and out. Put the turkey breast in a baking dish and let it rest in the refrigerator, uncovered, overnight or up to 24 hours.

2. Spit the turkey breast: One hour before cooking, remove the turkey breast from the refrigerator. Skewer the breast on the rotisserie spit, securing it with the spit forks. Let it rest at room temperature until it is time to cook.

3. Set up the grill: Set up the grill for indirect medium heat (325° to 350°F) with the drip pan in the middle of the grill and the heat on the sides. (Split the charcoal into two piles on the sides or turn on the burners on the edges the grill; see the Charcoal Grill Setup and Gas Grill Setup chapters for more details).

4. Cook the turkey breast: Put the spit on the grill, start the rotisserie spinning, and make sure the drip pan is centered under the turkey. Close the lid. If you are using a charcoal grill, add 16 unlit briquettes after an hour to keep the heat going. Cook until the turkey breast reaches 150°F in its thickest part (about 1 ¾ hours), then add 5 minutes more cooking time.

5. Carve and serve: Remove the turkey from the grill and remove the spit from the turkey. Let the turkey rest for 15 minutes before carving. Cut the breast halves from the keel bone and ribcage, then carve the breast into ¼-inch-thick slices. Arrange the turkey slices on a platter and serve.

TURKEY BREAST WITH ITALIAN-SPICED DRY BRINE

To perk up a bland turkey breast, I rub it with an Italian-inspired blend of coarsely ground spices. That blend includes a big dose of red pepper flakes and black pepper, adding a spicy kick to contrast with the neutral meat.

Ingredients

6-to-8-pound turkey breast

1 teaspoon black peppercorns

1 teaspoon fennel seeds

1 teaspoon coriander seeds

½ teaspoon red pepper flakes

4 teaspoons Diamond Crystal kosher salt or 1 tablespoon Morton's kosher salt (½ ounce)

Directions

1. Dry brine the turkey breast: Eight hours to 1 day before it is time to cook, pat the turkey breast dry with paper towels. Cut the extra skin away from the neck. Check inside the neck cavity, and discard any big pieces of fat. Coarsely grind together the peppercorns, fennel, coriander, and red pepper flakes, then stir in the salt. (I grind with a mortar and pestle or in an electric coffee mill that I only use for spice grinding.)

Gently work the skin loose from the turkey breast starting from the back of the bird, and rub 1 teaspoon of the brine directly on the meat. Pull the skin back into place, then sprinkle the rest of the brine over the turkey breast, inside and out. Put the turkey breast in a baking dish and let it rest in the refrigerator, uncovered, overnight or up to 24 hours.

Pull the skin back into place, then sprinkle the rest of the spice mix over the turkey breast, inside and out. Put the turkey breast in a baking dish and let it rest in the refrigerator overnight, or up to 24 hours.

2. Spit the turkey breast: One hour before cooking, remove the turkey breast from the refrigerator. Skewer the breast on the rotisserie spit, securing it with the spit forks. Let it rest at room temperature until it is time to cook.

3. Set up the grill: Set up the grill for indirect medium heat (325° to 350°F) with the drip pan in the middle of the grill and the heat on the sides. (Split the charcoal into two piles on the sides, or turn on the burners on the edges the grill; see the Charcoal Grill Setup and Gas Grill Setup chapters for more details).

4. Cook the turkey breast: Put the spit on the grill, start the rotisserie spinning, and make sure the drip pan is centered under the turkey. Close the lid. If you are using a charcoal grill, add 16 unlit briquettes after an hour to keep the heat going. Cook until the turkey breast reaches 150°F in its thickest part (about 1 ¾ hours), then add 5 minutes more cooking time.

5. Carve and serve: Remove the turkey from the grill and remove the spit from the turkey. Let the turkey rest for 15 minutes before carving. Cut the breast halves from the keel bone and ribcage, then carve the breast into ¼-inch-thick slices. Arrange the turkey slices on a platter and serve.

WET-BRINED TURKEY BREAST WITH GARLIC HERB PASTE

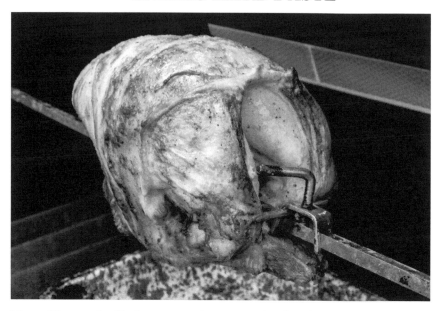

Now, I know I talk down wet brines in this book a lot, but if you're in a hurry, or if you love juicy breast meat, wet brines are the way to go. To punch up the flavor even more, I rub the turkey with an herb paste right before it goes on the grill.

Equipment

A container large enough to hold the turkey breast—I use an 8-quart covered food service container

Ingredients

Turkey and Brine

1 gallon cold water

¼ cup table salt or ½ cup kosher salt (3 ounces)

2 tablespoons light or dark brown sugar

6-to-8-pound turkey breast

Garlic Herb Paste

2 teaspoons minced fresh sage leaves

2 teaspoons minced fresh rosemary leaves

2 teaspoons minced fresh thyme leaves

2 minced cloves garlic

1 teaspoon kosher salt

½ teaspoon freshly ground black pepper

2 tablespoons olive oil

Directions

1. Brine the turkey breast: One to 8 hours before it is time to cook, pat the turkey breast dry with paper towels. Cut the extra skin away from the neck. Check inside the neck cavity and discard any big pieces of fat.

Pour the water into the container. Add the salt and sugar and stir until they dissolve. Submerge the turkey breast in the brine and refrigerate for at least 1 hour, preferably 4 to 8 hours.

2. Rub and spit the turkey breast: One hour before cooking, remove the turkey breast from the brine and pat dry with paper towels. Discard the brine.

Mix the sage, rosemary, thyme, garlic, salt, pepper, and olive oil in a small bowl. Gently work the skin loose from the turkey breast starting from the back of the bird, and rub 1 teaspoon of the herb paste directly on the meat. Pull the skin back into place, then spread the rest of the paste over the turkey breast, inside and out. Skewer the breast on the rotisserie spit, securing it with the spit forks. Let it rest at room temperature until it is time to cook.

3. Set up the grill: Set up the grill for indirect medium heat (325° to 350°F) with the drip pan in the middle of the grill and the heat on the sides. (Split the charcoal into two piles on the sides, or turn on the burners on the edges the grill; see the Charcoal Grill Setup and Gas Grill Setup chapters for more details).

4. Cook the turkey breast: Put the spit on the grill, start the rotisserie spinning, and make sure the drip pan is centered under the turkey. Close the lid. If you are using a charcoal grill, add 16 unlit briquettes after an hour to keep the heat going. Cook until the turkey breast reaches 150°F in its thickest part (about 1 ¾ hours), then add 5 minutes more cooking time.

5. Carve and serve: Remove the turkey from the grill and remove the spit from the turkey. Let the turkey rest for 15 minutes before carving. Cut the breast halves from the keel bone and ribcage, then carve the breast into ¼-inch-thick slices. Arrange the turkey slices on a platter and serve.

TURKEY BREAST WITH SMOKED PAPRIKA RUB

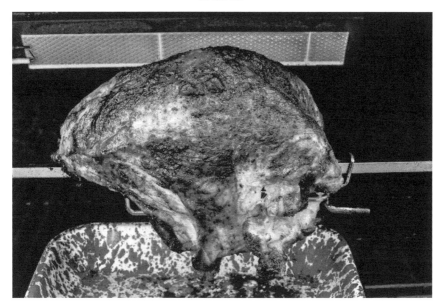

Smoked paprika is my secret weapon. When I first learned about Spanish pimentón, it was only available in expensive little blue tins. Now it's easy to find in the spice aisle of your grocery store. I even have a local source—an old-school Hungarian butcher who smokes paprika to use in his sausages, and sells both the smoked paprika and the sausages. If you can't find smoked paprika locally, substitute sweet paprika. Or look for it online—I like Penzeys for mail-order spices.

I'm using the spice rub as a quick flavor boost, but it can work as a dry brine—rub the turkey breast with it the night before cooking and refrigerate. Remove the turkey breast from the refrigerator about 1 hour before cooking to come to room temperature.

Ingredients

6-to-8-pound turkey breast

Smoked Paprika Rub

2 tablespoons paprika (preferably smoked Spanish paprika)

2 teaspoons ground coriander

1 teaspoon ground cumin

1 teaspoon freshly ground black pepper

½ teaspoon dry mustard powder

4 teaspoons Diamond Crystal kosher salt or 1 tablespoon Morton's kosher salt (½ ounce)

Directions

1. Rub and spit the turkey breast: One hour before cooking, pat the turkey breast dry with paper towels. Cut the extra skin away from the neck. Check inside the neck cavity and discard any big pieces of fat.

Mix the paprika, coriander, cumin, pepper, mustard, and salt in a small bowl. Gently work the skin loose from the turkey breast starting from the back of the bird, and spread 1 teaspoon of the rub directly on the meat. Pull the skin back into place, then sprinkle the rest of the rub over the turkey breast, inside and out, patting it gently to help it stick. Skewer the breast on the rotisserie spit, securing it with the spit forks. Let it rest at room temperature until it is time to cook.

2. Set up the grill: Set up the grill for indirect medium heat (325° to 350°F), with the drip pan in the middle of the grill and the heat on the sides. (Split the charcoal into two piles on the sides, or turn on the burners on the edges the grill; see the Charcoal Grill Setup and Gas Grill Setup chapters for more details).

3. Cook the turkey breast: Put the spit on the grill, start the rotisserie spinning, and make sure the drip pan is centered under the turkey.

Close the lid. If you are using a charcoal grill, add 16 unlit briquettes after an hour to keep the heat going. Cook until the turkey breast reaches 150°F in its thickest part (about 1 ¾ hours), then add 5 minutes more cooking time.

4. Carve and serve: Remove the turkey from the grill and remove the spit from the turkey. Let the turkey rest for 15 minutes before carving. Cut the breast halves from the keel bone and ribcage, then carve the breast into ¼-inch-thick slices. Arrange the turkey slices on a platter and serve.

Texas Hill Country Smoked Turkey Breast

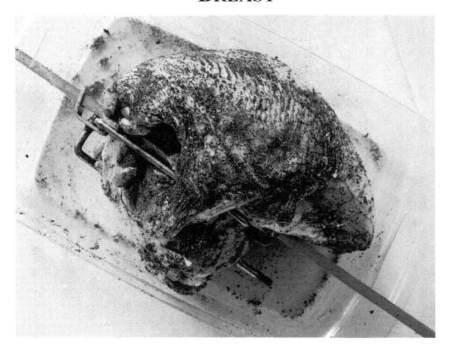

One of my favorite food tours was a trip to Austin, Texas. I was there for my day job, but my real goal was to visit every Texas barbecue joint I could. I was surprised at how many barbecue joints serve turkey breast, and how good it was. Texas pitmasters know more than just brisket.

The spice rub can work as a dry brine—rub the turkey breast with it the night before cooking and refrigerate. Remove the turkey breast from the refrigerator about one hour before cooking, to come to room temperature.

Equipment

2 fist-size chunks of smoking wood or 2 cups wood chips (oak or pecan)

Ingredients

6-to-8-pound turkey breast

1 fist sized chunk of smoking wood, or 2 cups wood chips (Oak or Pecan)

Texas Rub

4 teaspoons Diamond Crystal kosher salt or 1 tablespoon Morton's kosher salt (½ ounce)

2 tablespoons ground ancho chiles

2 teaspoons ground cumin

2 teaspoons freshly ground black pepper

Directions

1. Rub and spit the turkey breast: One hour before cooking, pat the turkey breast dry with paper towels. Cut the extra skin away from the neck. Check inside the neck cavity and discard any big pieces of fat.

Mix the salt, ground chiles, cumin, and pepper in a small bowl. Gently work the skin loose from the turkey breast starting from the back of the bird, and spread 1 teaspoon of the rub directly on the meat. Pull the skin back into place, then sprinkle the rest of the rub over the turkey breast, inside and out, patting it gently to help it stick. Skewer the breast on the rotisserie spit, securing it with the spit forks. Let it rest at room temperature until it is time to cook.

2. Set up the grill: Set up the grill for indirect medium heat (325° to 350°F) with the drip pan in the middle of the grill and the heat on the sides. (Split the charcoal into two piles on the sides, or turn on the burners on the edges the grill; see the Charcoal Grill Setup and Gas Grill Setup chapters for more details). Add the smoking wood to the fire right before adding the turkey breast.

3. Cook the turkey breast: Put the spit on the grill, start the rotisserie spinning, and make sure the drip pan is centered under the turkey. Close the lid. If you are using a charcoal grill, add 16 unlit briquettes after an hour to keep the heat going. Cook until the turkey breast reaches 150°F in its thickest part (about 1 ¾ hours), then add 5 minutes more cooking time.

4. Carve and serve: Remove the turkey from the grill and remove the spit from the turkey. Let the turkey rest for 15 minutes before carving. Cut the breast halves from the keel bone and ribcage, then carve the breast into ¼-inch-thick slices. Arrange the turkey slices on a platter and serve.

Turkey Breast With Honey-Bourbon Glaze

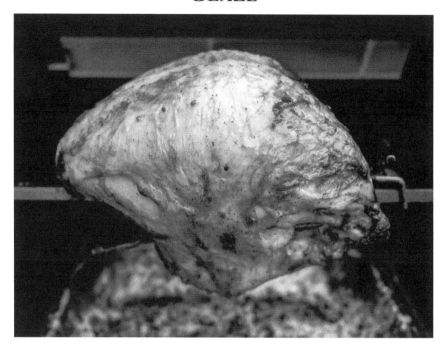

There's nothing like perking up a turkey breast with a sweet glaze. Of course, I had to add a little bourbon to the mix. I'm a combination of bourbon snob and cheapskate—if I'm drinking bourbon, I don't want any "stuff" in it other than a single ice cube, so I buy expensive small-batch bourbon for sipping. I don't want to waste the good stuff when I'm cooking, though; for cooking, I buy 50 ml mini bottles of cheap bourbon. If you're feeling adventurous, use actual honey bourbon in this recipe.

Equipment

2 fist-size chunks of smoking wood or 2 cups wood chips (oak or pecan)

Ingredients

6-to-8-pound turkey breast

4 teaspoons Diamond Crystal kosher salt or 1 tablespoon Morton's kosher salt (½ ounce)

Honey-Bourbon Glaze

½ cup honey

100 ml or ½ cup bourbon (use honey bourbon, if you have it)

1 teaspoon cayenne pepper (optional)

Directions

1. Dry-brine the turkey: Eight hours to 1 day before it is time to cook, pat the turkey breast with paper towels. Cut the extra skin away from the neck. Check inside the neck cavity and discard any big pieces of fat. Gently work the skin loose from the turkey breast, starting from the back of the bird, and rub 1 teaspoon of the salt directly on the breast meat. Pull the skin back into place, then sprinkle the rest of the salt all over the turkey breast, inside and out. Put the turkey breast in a baking dish and let it rest in the refrigerator, uncovered, overnight or up to 24 hours.

2. Spit the turkey breast: One hour before cooking, remove the turkey breast from the refrigerator. Skewer the breast on the rotisserie spit, securing it with the spit forks. Let it rest at room temperature until it is time to cook.

3. Set up the grill: Set up the grill for indirect medium heat (325° to 350°F), with the drip pan in the middle of the grill and the heat on the sides. (Split the charcoal into two piles on the sides, or turn on the burners on the edges the grill; see the Charcoal Grill Setup and Gas Grill Setup chapters for more details). Add the smoking wood to the fire right before adding the turkey breast.

4. Make the glaze: While the grill is heating, stir together the honey, bourbon, and cayenne in a small saucepan. Simmer over medium heat until reduced by half, about minutes. Remove from the heat.

5. Cook the turkey breast: Put the spit on the grill, start the rotisserie spinning, and make sure the drip pan is centered under the turkey. Close the lid. If you are using a charcoal grill, add 16 unlit briquettes after an hour to keep the heat going. After 1 ½ hours of cooking, brush the turkey breast with a layer of glaze, then brush every 5 minutes for the next 15 minutes. Cook until the turkey breast reaches 150°F in its thickest part (about 1 ¾ hours), then add 5 minutes more cooking time.

6. Carve and serve: Remove the turkey from the grill and remove the spit from the turkey. Brush with one last coat of glaze, then let the turkey rest for 15 minutes before carving. Cut the breast halves from the keel bone and ribcage, then carve the breast into ¼-inch-thick slices. Arrange the turkey slices on a platter and serve.

TURKEY BREAST MOLE

Turkey in mole poblano is Mexico's celebration meal. Sweet, spicy, and complex, a true mole poblano is an all-day affair—multiple days, actually—that will test your dedication to cooking. I've made a few moles in my day, and they're fantastic, but I am willing to take a shortcut in this case. (By the way, "mole" rhymes with "Olé," not the small furry rodent. Though my kids giggled all through dinner saying they were eating mole sauce.)

You can buy mole pastes at your local Mexican mercado or well-stocked gourmet food store - which do most of the cooking ahead of time. Doña Maria brand is widely available, and it is fine. My favorite brand of mole pastes is Seasons of My Heart, but I'm biased—I spent a week at their cooking school in Oaxaca. If you have a good mercardo, you'll have a variety of mole styles to choose from; any of them will work, but I prefer the dark moles with turkey. Look for a mole rojo, poblano, negro, or coloradito.

Ingredients

6-to-8-pound turkey breast

4 teaspoons Diamond Crystal kosher salt or 1 tablespoon Morton's kosher salt (½ ounce)

1 teaspoon ground ancho chiles

1 (8-ounce) jar mole paste

Toasted Sesame Seeds (optional)

Tortillas

Directions

1. Dry-brine the turkey: Eight hours to 1 day before it is time to cook, pat the turkey breast dry with paper towels. Mix the salt and ground chiles in a small bowl. Gently work the skin loose from the turkey breast, then rub 1 teaspoon of the brine directly on the breast meat. Pull the skin back into place, then sprinkle the rest of the brine all over the turkey breast, inside and out. Put the turkey breast in a baking dish and let it rest in the refrigerator, uncovered, overnight or up to 24 hours.

2. Spit the turkey breast: One hour before cooking, remove the turkey breast from the refrigerator. Skewer the breast on the rotisserie spit, securing it with the spit forks. Let it rest at room temperature until it is time to cook.

3. Set up the grill: Set up the grill for indirect medium heat (325° to 350°F), with the drip pan in the middle of the grill and the heat on the sides. (Split the charcoal into two piles on the sides, or turn on burners on the edges the grill; (see the Charcoal Grill Setup and Gas Grill Setup chapters for more details).

4. Cook the turkey breast: Put the spit on the grill, start the rotisserie spinning, and make sure the drip pan is centered under the turkey. Close the lid. If you are using a charcoal grill, add 16 unlit briquettes after an hour to keep the heat going. Cook until the turkey breast reaches 150°F in its thickest part (about 1 ¾ hours), then add 5 minutes more cooking time.

5. Cook the mole: While the turkey is cooking, prepare the mole sauce according to the package instructions. This usually means frying the paste in oil, then simmering with chicken broth. If you have Turkey Broth (Page 115) in the freezer, use it!

6. Carve and serve: Remove the turkey from the grill and remove the spit from the turkey. Let the turkey rest for 15 minutes before carving. Cut the breast halves from the keel bone and ribcage, then carve the breast into ¼-inch-thick slices. Put a few slices on a plate, ladle a generous amount of mole sauce over the top, sprinkle with sesame seeds, if you like, and serve with tortillas to mop up the sauce.

TURKEY LEGS BRINED AND HONEY GARLIC BASTED

Okay, you got me . . . this isn't a turkey breast recipe. But I had to include it. I love eating food off the bone. There is something primal about food with a built-in handle, and state fair turkey legs have always been a weakness of mine. Here's my version: sweet, tender, glazed drumsticks from the rotisserie.

Equipment

3 spit forks (2 drumsticks per fork)

A covered container large enough to hold all the drumsticks

6 small squares of aluminum foil

Ingredients

Brined Drumsticks

3 quarts water

¼ cup table salt or ½ cup kosher salt (3 ounces)

¼ cup light or dark brown sugar

6 Turkey Drumsticks

Baste

2 tablespoons vegetable oil

2 tablespoons (¼ stick) butter

3 tablespoons honey

1 tablespoon soy sauce

1 teaspoon Worcestershire sauce

1 tablespoon apple cider vinegar

2 cloves garlic, minced

3 or 4 sprigs of fresh herbs such as thyme, rosemary, marjoram, and/or oregano (optional)

Directions

1. Brine the drumsticks: One to 4 hours before it is time to cook, combine the water, salt, and sugar in the container and stir until the sugar and salt dissolve. Add the drumsticks, cover, and refrigerate.

2. Prepare the baste and herb brush: Put the oil, butter, honey, soy sauce, Worcestershire, vinegar, and garlic in a microwave-safe bowl and heat in the microwave for 1 minute, or until the butter melts and you can smell the garlic. Stir to mix. Tie the herb sprigs together at the base of the stem to make a brush. (You can use a regular basting brush instead.)

3. Spit the drumsticks: Run the spit through the narrowest part of the meat of one drumstick, at the middle of the bone, and secure the knob of the drumstick on the spit fork. Add a second drumstick to the same fork with the bone end pointing in the other direction in the same way, with the spit through the narrow part of the meat, fork through the thick part of the drumstick. Repeat, putting two drumsticks on each spit fork. Wrap the bone end of each drumstick with a small square of aluminum foil to keep it from burning. Let the drumsticks sit at room temperature while you prepare the grill.

4. Set up the grill: Set up the grill for indirect medium heat (325° to 350°F), with the drip pan in the middle of the grill and the heat on the sides. (Split the charcoal into two piles on the sides, or turn on burners on the edges the grill; see the Charcoal Grill Setup and Gas Grill Setup chapters for more details).

5. Cook the drumsticks: Put the spit on the grill, start the rotisserie spinning, and make sure the drip pan is centered under the drumsticks. Close the lid. After about 45 minutes of cooking, use the herb brush to brush a layer of baste on the legs, then brush every 5 minutes for the next 15 minutes. Cook until the drumsticks reach 175°F in their thickest part, about 1 hour.

5. Serve: Remove the spit from the grill and remove the legs from the spit. Arrange the legs on a platter. Brush the legs with one last coat of baste, then let them rest for 10 minutes before serving.

TURKEY SIDES

ROTISSERIE TURKEY 92

I need five things on Thanksgiving:

1. Turkey
2. Gravy
3. Potatoes
4. Stuffing
5. Squash

Oh, and of course a glass of wine or two—especially while I'm cooking.

Everything else is nice, but those five are mandatory or it's just not Thanksgiving.

I talked earlier about moving the turkey out of the kitchen and onto the grill; here I use the grill for some of the side dishes as well. I usually cook a big pan of stuffing under the turkey, and if I have two grills going, I use the second drip pan to make potatoes, sweet potatoes, or squash.

The downside to grilling turkey is the drippings in the pan are usually a mess—burnt and sooty—so I make my gravy ahead of time with the giblets and neck that came in the bird. This also moves the gravy outside of Turkey Day crunch time—it just needs to be reheated on the stovetop to serve.

Make-Ahead Giblet Gravy (With Drippings?)

Make-ahead gravy helps avoid the great Thanksgiving Time Crunch, when everything has to be cooking a half hour before dinner time.

You can pull that off with a dinner party for eight people—it makes for a harried cook, but it can be done. On Thanksgiving, when you're cooking for a big crowd? The last-minute rush is an invitation for disaster. (Especially when the whole family shows up, including all the aunts, uncles, and cousins, and you're cooking for 25 people.) There is only so much space in the oven, so many burners available, and the clock is always ticking. Giblet gravy can be made up to three days ahead, using the odd bits of turkey stuffed in the turkey's cavities. That way, there is one less thing to worry about on T-Day.

I am also a pressure cooker fanatic—I use it to speed up the turkey broth in the recipe. Don't worry, you can make the gravy without a pressure cooker. It just takes a lot longer.

Yield: 3 cups of gravy

Equipment

Large pot or pressure cooker

Fine-mesh strainer

Ingredients

1 tablespoon vegetable oil

Turkey neck, heart, gizzard, and butt, but skip the liver (see Notes)

1 medium onion, quartered

½ cup dry vermouth or dry white wine

2 sprigs fresh thyme

1 bay leaf

4 tablespoons (½ stick) butter

¼ cup all purpose flour

Salt and freshly ground black pepper

Pan drippings (optional)

Directions

1. Brown the turkey and aromatics: Heat the vegetable oil in the pot over medium-high heat until shimmering. Add the turkey pieces and onion and cook until browned, about 3 minutes. Flip and brown the other side, another 3 minutes. Add the vermouth and bring to a boil, then scrape any browned bits from the bottom of the pot. Add the thyme and bay leaf. Add 4 cups water if cooking in a pressure cooker or 5 cups if using a regular pot.

2. Cook the broth: If you're cooking the broth in a regular pot, bring it to a boil, reduce the heat to a low simmer, cover with a lid, and simmer for 4 hours.

If you're using a pressure cooker, lock the lid and bring to high pressure over high heat. Reduce the heat and cook at high pressure for 30 minutes. Remove the pressure cooker from the heat and let the pressure come down naturally, about 10 minutes.

3. Strain the broth: Strain the broth through a fine-mesh strainer, reserving the gizzard and heart and discarding the neck and the butt. When the giblets have cooled enough to handle, remove the gristle from the gizzard and finely dice the heart and gizzard. Set aside for later.

4. Make a light brown roux: Melt the butter in a saucepan over medium heat and wait for it to stop foaming. Whisk in the flour and cook, whisking constantly, until the flour is the color of peanut butter, about 3 minutes.

5. Make the gravy: Slowly pour the strained broth into the roux, whisking vigorously. Bring to a boil. Reduce the heat to a simmer and cook, stirring occasionally, until the gravy thickens and reduces by one-third, about 20 minutes.

Stir in the heart and gizzard pieces. Add salt and pepper to taste. Don't skip this step—the gravy needs salt to taste right. Keep adding salt until the gravy goes from watery to full-bodied.

6. Store the gravy: Let the gravy cool to room temperature, then store in the refrigerator in a sealed container for up to 3 days.

7. Reheat the gravy and serve: When it's time to use the gravy, bring to a boil over medium heat, stirring often, and boil for 1 minute. Check the pan drippings from the grill; if they're burnt, or full of charcoal ash, discard them. If not, use them: scrape them loose from the pan, then stir into the gravy. Serve.

Notes

Giblet gravy is three basic techniques strung together: First, make a broth using the giblets, neck, turkey butt, and some aromatics.

Second, make a light brown roux to thicken the broth into gravy. Finally, season to taste—the key to good gravy.

I don't use the turkey liver in my giblet gravy—I think it makes the gravy taste "livery." But I've heard from some readers who love the taste and can't believe I leave it out. Tastes differ, so use your own judgment on that one. If you do use it, add it with the other giblets when you're making the stock. When the stock is done, dice it and add it to the gravy with the rest of the diced giblets.

ROTISSERIE PAN STUFFING WITH CRANBERRIES AND APPLES

Why cook stuffing in the grill? Because, on Thanksgiving, it's one less thing to try to fit in the oven. The grill is already heated up for cooking the turkey; I slide the pan of stuffing in when it has about an hour left to cook. As a bonus, the stuffing picks up some drippings from the turkey.

Normally I'm a charcoal snob, but this recipe works better on the gas grill. The even heat of gas makes a great oven substitute. A charcoal grill tends to burn the stuffing around the edges and undercook the middle.

Equipment

11 by 15-inch disposable aluminum pan or 12 by 16-inch oval turkey roasting pan

Ingredients

8 tablespoons (1 stick) butter

2 large onions, diced

2 stalks celery, trimmed and diced

3 apples, peeled, cored, and diced (Granny Smith or other tart apple)

3 cloves garlic, minced

1 tablespoon Diamond Crystal kosher salt or 2 teaspoons fine sea salt

1 tablespoon fresh thyme leaves (or 1½ teaspoon dried thyme)

1 tablespoon minced fresh sage leaves, or 1 ½ teaspoons dried crumbled sage

2 pounds dried bread cubes (look for bags in the bakery of your local grocery store)

1 cup dried cranberries (5 ounces)

1 quart chicken broth or Turkey Broth (Page 115)

2 teaspoons freshly ground black pepper

2 eggs, beaten

Directions

ROTISSERIE PAN STUFFING WITH CRANBERRIES AND APPLES 99

1. Sauté the aromatics: Melt the butter in a large frypan over medium-high heat. Add the onions, celery, apples, and garlic, then sprinkle with 2 teaspoons of the salt. Sauté until the onions are soft, about 5 minutes. Stir in the thyme and sage, and cook until you smell the herbs, about another minute. Remove from the heat.

2. Mix the stuffing: Put half the bread and all the cranberries in a large bowl. Scrape the aromatics into the bowl, then stir until everything is evenly mixed. Pour in half the broth, add the remaining 1 teaspoon salt and the pepper, and stir until all the bread is damp. Stir in the rest of the bread and broth in batches, adding more when the stuffing compacts enough to fit in the bowl. Stir in the eggs. Pour the stuffing into the pan. Crimp a sheet of aluminum foil over the pan.

3. Cook the stuffing: If you're cooking the stuffing on the grill under the turkey, cut slits in the foil so the turkey drippings can drip through into the stuffing. When you figure the turkey has about 1 hour left to cook, swap out the drip pan for the pan of stuffing. If the drippings in the drip pan aren't burnt, pour them onto the foil covering the stuffing, to drip through the slits. Cook the stuffing covered for 45 minutes. Remove the foil and cook until the stuffing is browned and crispy on top and the stuffing registers 150°F in the middle, about 15 minutes more.

If you're cooking the stuffing in the oven, preheat the oven to 350°F. Cook the stuffing covered for 45 minutes. Remove the foil and cook until the stuffing is browned and crispy on top and registers 150°F in the middle, about 15 minutes more.

4. Serve: Carefully remove the stuffing from the oven or grill. Scoop the stuffing into a serving dish. If the stuffing needs to sit while you carve the turkey, cover the dish with foil to keep it warm.

ROTISSERIE PAN CHESTNUT STUFFING

Chestnut stuffing. It just sounds like a Charles Dickens holiday special, doesn't it? Here's an Italian-style chestnut stuffing, adapted for the rotisserie pan from a recipe by Melissa Hamilton and Christopher Hirsheimer, authors of the wonderful Canal House Cooking series of cookbooks.

Equipment

11 by 15-inch disposable aluminum pan or 12 by 16-inch oval turkey roasting pan

Ingredients

8 tablespoons (1 stick) butter

2 large onions, diced

2 stalks celery, trimmed and diced

½ cup diced prosciutto (8 ounces)

2 cloves garlic, minced

2 teaspoons kosher salt

16 ounces (three 150 gram bags) peeled, roasted chestnuts, chopped into large chunks

2 teaspoons minced fresh rosemary leaves

1 cup raisins

2 pounds dried bread cubes (look for bags in the bakery of your local grocery store)

1 cup minced fresh parsley leaves

1 quart chicken broth or Turkey Broth (Page 115)

2 teaspoons freshly ground black pepper

Directions

1. Sauté the aromatics: Melt the butter in a large frypan over medium-high heat. Add the onions, celery, prosciutto, and garlic, then sprinkle with 1 teaspoon of the salt. Sauté until the onions are soft, about 5 minutes. Stir in the chestnuts and rosemary and cook for 1 minute more. Remove from the heat.

2. Mix the stuffing: Put half the bread and all the raisins in a large bowl. Scrape the aromatics and chestnuts into the bowl, then stir until everything is evenly mixed. Pour in half the broth, add the remaining 1 teaspoon salt and the pepper, and stir until all the bread is damp. Stir in the rest of the bread and broth in batches, adding more when the stuffing compacts enough to fit in the bowl. Pour the stuffing into the foil pan. Crimp a sheet of aluminum foil over the pan.

3. Cook the stuffing: If you're cooking the stuffing on the grill under the turkey, cut slits in the foil so the turkey drippings can drip through into the stuffing. When you figure the turkey has about 1 hour left to cook, swap out the drip pan for the pan full of stuffing. If the drippings in the drip pan aren't burnt, pour them onto foil covering the stuffing, to drip through the slits into the stuffing. Cook the stuffing covered for 45 minutes. Remove the foil and cook until the stuffing is browned and crispy on top and the stuffing registers 150°F in the middle, about 15 minutes more.

If you're cooking the stuffing in the oven, preheat the oven to 350°F. Cook the stuffing covered for 45 minutes. Remove the foil and cook until the stuffing is browned and crispy on top and registers 150°F in the middle, about 15 minutes more.

4. Serve: Carefully remove the stuffing from the oven or grill. Scoop the stuffing into a serving dish. If the stuffing needs to sit while you carve the turkey, cover the dish with foil to keep it warm.

Rotisserie Pan Cornbread Dressing

A friend who spent years in New Orleans challenged me after I posted yet another Thanksgiving stuffing recipe.

That stuffing looks good—but you have to try cornbread dressing.

As a Yankee, I had never heard of such a thing, but cornbread and sausage? Sounded like a great combination to me. I tried it, and guess what—they do know a thing or two about food down in N'awlins.

My only problem was my family's traditionalists. Cornbread dressing was fine, and they enjoyed it, but then they asked where the "real" stuffing was. Sometimes you can't fight tradition . . .

Equipment

11 by 15-inch disposable aluminum pan or 12 by 16-inch oval turkey roasting pan

Ingredients

4 tablespoons (½ stick) butter

2 onions, minced

2 stalks celery, trimmed and minced

1 red bell pepper, seeded and minced

2 or 3 teaspoons kosher salt

1 pound sage sausage (bulk or links; remove the casing from links)

¼ cup minced fresh parsley leaves

2 pounds stale cornbread, cut into 1-inch cubes (8 to 10 cups)

1 quart chicken broth or Turkey Broth (Page 115)

2 teaspoons freshly ground black pepper

2 eggs, beaten

Directions

1. Sauté the aromatics: Melt the butter in a large frypan over medium-high heat. Add the onions, celery, and bell pepper, then sprinkle with 2 teaspoons salt. Sauté until the onions are soft, about 5 minutes.

2. Brown the sausage: Add the sausage to the aromatics and cook, breaking the sausage into bite-size pieces, until the sausage is no longer pink, about 5 minutes. Stir in the parsley. Remove from the heat.

3. Mix the stuffing: Put half the cornbread in a large bowl. Scrape the aromatics and sausage into the bowl, then stir until everything is evenly mixed. Pour in half the broth and add the pepper. Add 1 teaspoon salt if using homemade broth. Stir until all the cornbread in the bowl is damp and compacted. Stir in the rest of the cornbread and broth in batches. Stir in the eggs. Pour the dressing into the pan. Crimp a sheet of aluminum foil over the pan.

4. Cook the stuffing: If you're cooking the dressing on the grill under the turkey, cut slits in the foil so the turkey drippings can drip through into the stuffing. When you figure the turkey has about 1 hour left to cook, swap out the drip pan for the pan of dressing. If the drippings in the drip pan aren't burnt, pour them onto the foil covering the dressing, to drip through the slits. Cook the dressing for 45 minutes. Remove the foil and cook until the dressing is browned and crispy on top and registers 150°F in the middle, about 15 minutes more.

If you're cooking the dressing in the oven, preheat the oven to 350°F. Cook the dressing covered for 45 minutes. Remove the foil and cook until the dressing is browned and crispy on top and registers 150°F in the middle, about 15 minutes more.

5. **Serve:** Carefully remove the dressing from the oven or grill. Scoop the dressing into a serving dish. If the dressing needs to sit while you carve the turkey, cover the dish with foil to keep it warm.

ROTISSERIE PAN SWEET POTATOES

Sweet potatoes come out of the drip pan browned and sweet, and they're a natural for the Thanksgiving table. All they need is precooking in the microwave—they need that head start so they cook through on the grill before they start to burn on the outside. If you are looking for an easy rotisserie side dish, one that isn't the "same old potatoes," give these a try.

Equipment

Grill with Rotisserie attachment (I used a Weber Summit with an infrared rotisserie burner. Here is the current version of my grill.)

9 by 12-inch foil pan

Ingredients

1 pound (2 large) sweet potatoes

1 teaspoon kosher salt

½ teaspoon freshly ground black pepper

1 teaspoon vegetable oil

Directions

1. Precook the sweet potatoes: Peel the sweet potatoes, cut in half lengthwise, then cut crosswise into ½-inch-thick slices. Put the slices in a microwave-safe bowl and toss with the salt, pepper, and vegetable oil until evenly coated. Cover the bowl with plastic wrap and microwave on high for 5 minutes.

2. Drip-pan roast the sweet potatoes: When you figure the turkey has about 30 minutes left to cook, carefully pour the sweet potatoes into the drip pan and spread them into an even layer. Cook until the sweet potatoes are browned and crispy on the top, about 30 minutes, stirring the potatoes if they are not browning evenly.

3. Serve: Transfer the sweet potatoes from the drip pan to a serving dish with a slotted spoon, leaving as much of the cooking fat behind as possible. Serve.

ROTISSERIE DRIP PAN SPIRAL POTATOES

I was inspired by the spiral skillet potatoes recipes I saw popping up all over the Internet—especially on Jeffrey B. Rogers's "The Culinary Fanatic" Facebook page. Think of potatoes au gratin or French-style pommes Anna, but in the drip pan on your grill. The only hard part of this recipe is thin-slicing the potatoes. If you have good knife skills, you're ready to go; if not, get a V-slicer or mandoline to make quick work of the potatoes.

Equipment

9 by 13-inch disposable aluminum or other grill-safe pan

Ingredients

1 tablespoon olive oil

3 pounds russet potatoes, scrubbed, sliced ¼ inch thick (discard the small end pieces)

4 tablespoons unsalted butter, cut into small cubes

2 teaspoons kosher salt

1 teaspoon freshly ground black pepper

½ cup shredded Colby-Jack cheese

Directions

1. Arrange the potatoes in the pan: Coat the bottom of the pan with the oil. Shingle the potatoes in a spiral around the pan. (To speed up the shingling, I do one potato at a time—I pick up a sliced potato, fan it out, and set it in the pan as the next part of the spiral.) Sprinkle the potatoes with the salt and pepper, then dot with the butter. Crimp a sheet of aluminum foil over the pan and cut slits in the foil so the turkey drippings can drip through into the potatoes.

2. Cook the potatoes: When you figure the turkey has about 1 ½ hours left to cook, swap out the drip pan for the pan of potatoes. Cook covered for 1 hour. Remove the foil and cook until the potatoes are browning on top, about 25 minutes more. Sprinkle the cheese over the potatoes and let it melt and bubble, about 5 minutes more.

3. Serve: Remove the pan from the grill and let it cool for about 5 minutes. Carefully work a spatula under the potatoes, lifting them loose from the pan. Slide the potatoes onto a large cutting board and slice into serving-size squares.

ROTISSERIE PAN BUTTERNUT SQUASH

I take the easy way out with this recipe. Around Thanksgiving, my grocery store sells tubs of peeled, cubed butternut squash. Buying it that way feels like I'm getting away with something—but it's much easier than peeling and seeding squash myself. That said, those tubs of squash seem to get soggy pretty quick, so for the freshest squash, take the time to peel and seed it yourself.

Equipment

9 by 13-inch disposable aluminum or other grill-safe pan

Ingredients

2 large butternut squash, peeled, seeded and cut into 1-inch cubes, or 3 pounds of pre-peeled and cubed squash

2 teaspoons kosher salt

½ teaspoon freshly ground black pepper

½ teaspoon freshly grated nutmeg

1 tablespoon vegetable oil

Directions

1. Prep the squash: Put the squash in the pan, sprinkle with the salt, pepper, and nutmeg, then drizzle with the vegetable oil. Toss the squash to coat, then spread into a single layer. Crimp a sheet of aluminum foil over the pan and cut slits in the foil so the turkey drippings can drip through into the squash.

2. Roast the squash: When you figure the turkey has about 45 minutes left to cook, swap out the drip pan for the pan of squash. Cook the squash covered for 15 minutes, then remove the foil and cook until the squash are browning on top and easily pierced with a paring knife, about 30 minutes more.

3. Serve: Transfer the squash from the pan to a serving dish with a slotted spoon, leaving as much of the cooking fat behind as possible.

TURKEY SOUP

Save the bones!

My favorite Thanksgiving tradition doesn't happen on Thanksgiving. It happens the day after, when I turn the turkey carcass into a big pot of soup.

Now, I know some people think leftovers are boring. Soup, however, is different. It's making something new from the remains of the last meal.

This chapter is my basic broth recipe, followed by some suggestions for soups. Treat these as suggestions and add what you like—I hope these recipes inspire you to find your own favorite turkey soup, and break out of the Thanksgiving leftover rut.

TURKEY BROTH

The key to turkey soup is is homemade turkey broth. It is kitchen alchemy: Take the bones with some meat still clinging to them and simmer them in water until they give up their flavor and body. Strain out the bones, and what's left is liquid gold—the best soup base you'll ever have, full of meaty goodness.

Even better? A turkey has enough bones to make a big batch, about 6 quarts. Two quarts of broth makes a large pot of soup, so you should have enough for three meals. Freeze the broth in 1-quart containers, and you can use it months later—there's nothing like a January soup with homemade broth as the base.

Equipment

A large pot with a lid, a pressure cooker, or a slow cooker

Ingredients

Bones from a rotisserie turkey, with clinging meat

1 cup white wine (optional)

2 medium onions, peeled

2 large carrots, peeled

2 stalks celery, trimmed

6 cloves garlic, peeled

2 bay leaves

1 tablespoon Diamond Crystal kosher salt or 1½ teaspoons table salt

6 quarts water, or enough to cover the ingredients

Directions

1. Make the broth: *If you're using a regular pot,* put the turkey bones and white wine in the pot over high heat and bring to a boil. Reduce the heat and simmer while you chop the onions, carrots, and celery. Add them to the bones and wine. Add the garlic, bay leaves, and salt. Add the water; if it doesn't cover the turkey bones, add more until everything is covered by 1 inch of water. Cover the pot, increase the heat to high, and bring to a boil. Reduce the heat to a simmer, set the lid slightly ajar, and simmer for 4 hours.

If you're using a pressure cooker, put the turkey bones and white wine in the pot. (If you have a small pressure cooker, you may have to break the carcass into a few pieces to get it to fit.) Bring to a boil over high heat, then reduce the heat and simmer the wine while you chop the onions, carrots, and celery. Add them to the bones and wine. Add the garlic, bay leaves, and salt. Add the water; if it doesn't cover the turkey bones, add more until everything is just covered. Lock the lid on the pressure cooker, increase the heat to high, and bring the cooker up to high pressure. Cook at high pressure for 1 hour. Remove the pot from the heat. Allow the pressure to release naturally, usually about 20 minutes, then unlock the lid.

If you're using a slow cooker, put the turkey bones and white wine in the slow cooker. (If you have a small slow cooker, you may have to break the carcass into a few pieces to get it to fit.) Chop the onions, carrots, and celery and add them to the bones and wine along with the garlic, bay leaves, salt, and water, If the water doesn't cover the turkey bones, add more until everything is just covered. Cover the slow cooker, set it to low, and cook for 8 hours.

2. Strain the broth: Using a slotted spoon, scoop out and discard as much of the solids as possible. Pour the broth through a fine-mesh strainer into another large pot, and throw away everything caught by the strainer.

3. Use or freeze the broth: Use the broth immediately, or freeze for later use. I pour the broth into 1-quart containers for freezing. You can also refrigerate the broth to use within 2 days.

Note:

To defat the broth: After you strain the broth, refrigerate it overnight. The fat will float to the surface and form a hard cap. Remove the fat cap from the top of the broth with a slotted spoon, and you have mostly fat-free broth. around Thanksgiving, it's colder outside than it is in my refrigerator, so I do this by putting the covered pot of strained broth out on my back porch overnight. (My Samoan lawyer would like to add that you should only do this if the temperature will stay below 40°F the entire time.)

TURKEY NOODLE SOUP

Every year, I make this recipe the day after Thanksgiving. It's quick to throw together and a good way to relax the day after the festivities—and after a morning of Black Friday shopping.

Ingredients

1 tablespoon vegetable oil

1 medium onion, diced

1 medium carrot, peeled and diced

1 stalk celery, trimmed and diced

1 sprig fresh thyme or 1 teaspoon dried thyme

½ teaspoon Diamond Crystal kosher salt, plus more for seasoning (see Note)

8 cups (2 quarts) Turkey Broth (Page 115)

2 cups large dried egg noodles

2 cups shredded leftover turkey

1 or 2 dashes of hot sauce or cider vinegar (see Note)

Freshly ground black pepper

Directions

1. Sauté the aromatics: In a 4-quart or larger pot, heat the oil over medium-high heat until shimmering. Add the onion, carrot, celery, and thyme, sprinkle with the salt, and sauté until the onion is just starting to brown, about 5 minutes.

2. Make the soup: Add the broth, raise the heat to high, and boil for 1 minute. Stir in the noodles and turkey. Bring the soup back to a simmer, then reduce the heat and simmer for 10 minutes, or the cooking time from the bag of noodles, until the noodles are tender.

3. Season and serve: Add a dash of hot sauce, then add salt and pepper to taste. The soup will need a lot of salt, because there is very little salt in the broth. When you add salt, taste as you go until the flavor goes from flat to full-bodied and you can just taste a hint of salt on the tip of your tongue. (I usually add 2 teaspoons kosher salt to 2 quarts broth.) Ladle into soup bowls and serve.

Note

Tasting and seasoning soup is not optional! Soup needs seasoning or it is not done. Taste it—does the soup seem bland? Add salt until it goes from watery to full-bodied with a hint of sweetness. Add pepper, too. Hot sauce adds heat and acid to pick up the other up the flavors; if you can't stand the heat, add a splash of cider vinegar instead.

Turkey Soup With Rice

Cooking once, cooking twice, cooking turkey soup with rice. (Apologies to Maurice Sendak.) This turkey soup is for my wife; she grew up eating chicken soup with rice and singing the Carole King song. Here's my Thanksgiving leftovers version.

In the recipe I use uncooked green beans, but if you have cooked beans left over from Thanksgiving dinner, add them at the last minute so they warm up but don't cook to mush.

Ingredients

1 tablespoon vegetable oil

1 medium onion, peeled and cut into ½-inch dice

1 large carrot, peeled and cut into ½-inch thick rounds

1 stalk celery, trimmed and cut into ½-inch dice

½ teaspoon Diamond Crystal kosher salt or ¼ teaspoon table salt

1 teaspoon Italian seasoning, or dried basil, thyme, and/or oregano

½ teaspoon red pepper flakes

2 cloves garlic, peeled and crushed

8 cups (2 quarts) Turkey Broth (Page 115)

2 cups cooked white or brown rice

2 cups cubed cooked turkey meat (1-inch cubes)

8 ounces green beans, trimmed and cut in half crosswise (1 cup)

1 red bell pepper, seeded and cut into 1-inch squares

Splash of balsamic vinegar

Freshly ground black pepper

Directions

1. Sauté the aromatics: In a 4-quart or larger pot, heat the oil over medium-high heat until shimmering. Add the onion, carrot, and celery, and sprinkle with the Italian seasoning, red pepper flakes and salt. Sauté until the onion is just starting to brown, about 5 minutes. Add the garlic and sauté until you can smell the garlic, about 2 minutes more.

2. Make the soup: Add the broth, raise the heat to high, and boil for 1 minute. Stir in the rice, turkey, beans, and bell pepper. Bring back to a simmer, then reduce the heat and simmer for 10 minutes, until everything is heated through.

3. Season and serve: Add the vinegar, then add salt and black pepper to taste. The soup will need a lot of salt, because there is very little salt in the broth. When you add salt, taste as you go until the flavor goes from flat to full-bodied and you can just taste a hint of salt on the tip of your tongue. (I usually add 2 teaspoons kosher salt to 2 quarts broth.) Ladle into soup bowls and serve.

ITALIAN TURKEY SOUP WITH CHICKPEAS AND VEGETABLES

After I make my traditional American turkey soup, I like to experiment with the rest of the broth. Here is one of my favorites, a southern Italian–inspired soup with prosciutto, chickpeas, and spinach. Use lots of freshly ground pepper when you season—it's a very Italian thing to do.

Ingredients

1 tablespoon vegetable oil

1 medium onion, chopped into ½-inch chunks

2 carrots, peeled and chopped into ½-inch chunks

1 stalk celery, trimmed and chopped into ½-inch chunks

1 ounce prosciutto (about 5 slices), cut crosswise into ¼-inch slivers

½ teaspoon kosher salt, plus more for seasoning

2 cloves garlic, minced

1 sprig fresh thyme

1 sprig fresh rosemary

1 sprig fresh sage

½ cup white wine

8 cups (2 quarts) Turkey Broth (Page 115)

2 cups shredded cooked turkey

1 (15-ounce) can diced tomatoes, drained

1 (15-ounce) can chickpeas, drained

1 handful (about 1 cup) baby spinach leaves

Splash of balsamic vinegar

Freshly ground black pepper

Grated parmesan cheese, for serving

Directions

1. Sauté the aromatics: In a 4-quart or larger pot, heat the oil over medium-high heat until shimmering. Add the onion, carrot, celery, and prosciutto, and sprinkle with the salt. Sauté until the vegetables are soft and the prosciutto is getting crisp, about 5 minutes. Add the garlic and herb sprigs and sauté until you can smell the garlic, about 2 minutes more.

2. Make the soup: Raise the heat to high and pour in the white wine. Stir the aromatics into the wine, bring to a boil, and boil for 1 minute. Add the turkey broth and boil for 1 minute more. Stir in the turkey, tomatoes, and chickpeas. Bring back to a simmer, then reduce the heat and simmer for 10 minutes. Fish out the herb sprigs. Add the spinach and simmer until the spinach wilts, about 1 minute.

3. Season and serve: Add the vinegar, then add salt and pepper to taste. (The soup will need a lot of salt, because there is very little salt in the broth. When you add salt, taste as you go until the flavor goes from flat to full-bodied and you can just taste a hint of salt on the tip of your tongue. (I usually add 2 teaspoons kosher salt to 2 quarts broth.) Ladle into soup bowls, top with the cheese, and serve.

Turkey Tortilla Soup (Sopa De Tortilla)

I spent a week at Seasons of My Heart cooking school in Oaxaca, and I was surprised by soup. It was everywhere, served with almost every meal; if there wasn't a cup of broth, then we weren't done eating. Even roadside taco stands offered a cup of broth as an option with your tacos.

Tortilla soup is the Mexican soup that has broken through in America. Why? Because it takes our idea of chicken noodle soup, and reflects it back, full of Mexican flavors. The recipe calls for frying your own tortilla strips - the perfect use for leftover corn tortillas - but if you're in a hurry, substitute tortilla chips.

Ingredients

½ cup vegetable oil, or 1 tablespoon if using tortilla chips

6 tortillas, cut into ½-inch-wide strips, or 1 cup crumbled tortilla chips

1 medium onion, diced

½ teaspoon kosher salt, plus more for seasoning

6 cloves garlic, minced

1 (15-ounce) can crushed tomatoes (use fire-roasted crushed tomatoes, if you can find them)

8 cups (2 quarts) Turkey Broth (Page 115)

Freshly ground black pepper

Additions and Toppings

2 cups shredded cooked turkey

4 ounces queso fresco or farmer cheese, cut into ½-inch cubes (about 1 cup)

2 avocados, pitted, peeled, and cut into ½-inch cubes

2 canned chipotle chiles, minced, with 1 teaspoon adobo sauce, or 2 jalapeño peppers, minced

½ cup minced fresh cilantro

Limes, cut into wedges

Directions

1. Fry the tortilla strips: In a 4-quart or larger pot, heat ½ cup oil over medium-high heat until shimmering. Add half the tortilla strips and fry until golden brown, about 5 minutes; transfer the fried strips to a paper towel–lined plate to drain. Repeat with the remaining strips. Skip this step if you're using tortilla chips.

2. Sauté the aromatics: Pour out all but 1 tablespoon of the oil from the pot and turn the heat down to medium. (Or pour the tablespoon of oil into the pot and heat over medium heat.) Add the onion and sprinkle with the salt. Sauté until the onion starts to brown around the edges, about 5 minutes. Add the garlic and sauté until you can smell garlic, about 2 minutes more. Add the tomatoes and cook, stirring and scraping the bottom of the pot often, until the tomatoes thicken up, about 10 minutes.

3. Make the soup: Add the broth and scrape the bottom of the pot carefully to make sure no tomatoes are sticking. Raise the heat to high and boil for 1 minute. Reduce the heat and simmer for 15 minutes.

4. Season: Add salt and pepper to taste. (The soup will need a lot of salt, because there is very little salt in the broth. When you add salt, taste as you go until the flavor goes from flat to full-bodied and you can just taste a hint of salt on the tip of your tongue. (I usually add 2 teaspoons kosher salt to 2 quarts broth.)

5. Build the soup bowls and serve: In the bottom of each bowl, put some shredded turkey, a few cubes of cheese, a few cubes of avocado, and a teaspoon of minced chipotle. Ladle some soup into the bowl, sprinkle cilantro and fried tortilla strips on top, and serve. Pass lime wedges at the table.

TURKEY MISO NOODLE SOUP

Now we'll take our turkey soup to the Far East, Japanese style, with miso and udon noodles. You can find miso—a thick, fermented soybean paste—in tubs in the refrigerated section of well-stocked grocery stores. Or make a trip to your local Asian market. Don't skip the miso—it is a fabulous flavor enhancer, adding depth and body to the soup.

Note that miso clumps up if you add it directly to the soup. Stir it with a little of the broth first to make a slurry, then stir that into the soup. If you can find a bottle of liquid miso—I like Miso and Easy brand—you can add it straight to the pot.

Ingredients

8 ounces dried udon noodles or 12 ounces fresh noodles

1 tablespoon vegetable oil

1 medium onion, sliced thin

8 ounces shiitake or portobello mushrooms (caps only), sliced

1 clove garlic, peeled and crushed

8 cups (2 quarts) Turkey Broth (Page 115)

2 cups cubed cooked turkey breast

2 tablespoons miso (preferably white miso)

Salt

Toppings

½ small head Napa cabbage, sliced thin

1 large carrot, peeled and sliced thin

1 red bell pepper, seeded and sliced thin

1 serrano or jalapeño chile, sliced thin

2 green onions (scallions), trimmed and sliced thin

Directions

1. Cook the noodles: Cook the udon noodles in boiling water according to the package directions. Drain and rinse with cold water; set aside to use as a topping.

2. Sauté the aromatics: In a 4-quart or larger pot, heat the oil over medium-high heat until shimmering. Add the onion, mushrooms, and garlic. Sauté until the onions and mushrooms are browning around the edges, about 8 minutes.

3. Make the soup: Add the broth, raise the heat to high, and boil for 1 minute. Stir in the turkey. Bring the soup back to a simmer, then reduce the heat and simmer for 10 minutes, until the turkey is heated through.

4. Season: Put the miso in a small bowl and ladle in a cup of the broth. Whisk the miso and broth until the miso is completely dissolved, then stir it into the soup. Add salt to taste. (The soup will need salt—but not as much as the other soups in this chapter, because miso is salty—

because there is very little salt in the broth. When you add salt, taste as you go until the flavor goes from flat to full-bodied and you can just taste a hint of salt on the tip of your tongue. Here, I usually add 1 teaspoon kosher salt to 2 quarts broth.)

5. Let everyone build their own soup: Ladle the soup into bowls and serve with the toppings on the table so everyone can personalize their own bowl of soup.

ABOUT THE AUTHOR

Hi! I'm Mike Vrobel, indie cookbook author and food writer at DadCooksDinner.com.

Thank you for reading Rotisserie Turkey Grilling. I had a great time cooking, testing, tweaking, and photographing the book in your hands. If you have a minute, can you please review Rotisserie Turkey Grilling? Online reviews are the lifeblood of independent books like this one. Of course, my ego prefers five-star reviews, but any review is helpful.

Enjoyed this book? If you're looking for more rotisserie recipes, check out my Rotisserie Grilling and Rotisserie Chicken Grilling cookbooks at DadCooksDinner.com/Books.

Comments? Questions? Visit my blog, DadCooksDinner.com, and subscribe for food writing and recipes three times a week.

Mike Vrobel

October 2015

BIBLIOGRAPHY AND SUGGESTED READING

Everything I do is built on the shoulders of those who came before me. Here is the food writing that influenced this book:

Rotisserie Recipes

Parsons, Russ. "It's Roasting Outside." *Los Angeles Times*. 16 July 2003.

Purviance, Jamie. *Weber's Big Book of Grilling*. Oxmoor, 2001.

Purviance, Jamie. *Weber's Real Grilling*. Oxmoor, 2005.

Purviance, Jamie. *Weber's Charcoal Grilling*. Oxmoor, 2007.

Purviance, Jamie. *Weber's Way to Grill*. Oxmoor, 2009.

Raichlen, Steven. *How To Grill*. Workman, 2001.

Raichlen, Steven. *Beer Can Chicken*. Workman, 2002.

Raichlen, Steven. *BBQ USA*. Workman, 2003.

Raichlen, Steven. *The Barbecue! Bible*. Workman, 2008.

Raichlen, Steven. *Planet Barbecue!* Workman, 2010.

Steingarten, Jeffrey. "As the Spit Turns." *It Must've Been Something I Ate*. Knopf, 2002.

Vrobel, Mike. *Rotisserie Grilling*. House Sparrow Publishing, 2012.

Vrobel, Mike. *Rotisserie Chicken Grilling*. House Sparrow Publishing, 2014.

General Cooking Information

Anderson, Pam. How to Cook Without a Book. Clarkson Potter, 2000.

Bayless, Rick. Rick Bayless's Mexican Kitchen. Scribner, 1996.

Brown, Alton. Good Eats. Food Network, 1999-2012.

Hamilton, Melissa and Hirsheimer, Christopher. Canal House Cooking, Volumes 1 to 8. Canal House, 2009-present.

Kimball, Christopher, et al. Cooks Illustrated Magazine. Boston Common Press, 1993-present.

Lang, Mike. AnotherPintPlease.com, 2006-present. <http://www.anotherpintplease.com/>

Lopez-Alt, J. Kenji. "The Food Lab." SeriousEats.com, 2009-present. <http://www.seriouseats.com/the-food-lab>

McGee, Harold. On Food and Cooking. Scribner, 2004.

Page, Karen and Andrew Dornenburg. The Flavor Bible. Little, Brown, 2008.

Rodgers, Judy. The Zuni Cafe Cookbook. W. W. Norton, 2002.

Ruhlman, Michael. Ratio. Scribner, 2009.

Trilling, Susana. Seasons Of My Heart: A Culinary Journey through Oaxaca, Mexico. Ballantine, 1999.

ROTISSERIE TURKEY 134

25368593R00080

Made in the USA
Middletown, DE
27 October 2015